Anonymous

A list of the sheriffs of Cardiganshire, from A.D. 1539 to A.D.

1868

With genealogical and historical notes

Anonymous

A list of the sheriffs of Cardiganshire, from A.D. 1539 to A.D. 1868
With genealogical and historical notes

ISBN/EAN: 9783337264840

Printed in Europe, USA, Canada, Australia, Japan

Cover: Foto ©ninafisch / pixelio.de

More available books at **www.hansebooks.com**

OF THE

SHERIFFS OF CARDIGANSHIRE,

FROM A.D. 1539 TO A.D. 1868,

WITH

Genealogical and Historical Notes.

BY

JOHN ROLAND PHILLIPS,

AUTHOR OF THE "HISTORY OF CILGERRAN," &c.

CARMARTHEN:

PUBLISHED BY MORGAN & DAVIES, "WELSHMAN" PRINTING OFFICE.

1868.

WHILE the antiquity and importance of the office of Sheriff is generally admitted, there are on this, as on every other question in the least involved in obscurity by reason of its ancientness, various opinions as to its origin and derivation; but the most probable and best received opinion is that it is an office of Saxon origin, and that it dates from the time when good King Alfred bore the sceptre.

This king, whose wisdom, considering the age in which he lived, and the consequent disadvantages he laboured under, cannot fail even now to enlist our admiration, for the better government of this country, and that the administration of justice should be placed on a just and fair basis, caused the whole country over which he had dominion to be divided into tithings, hundreds, and shires, over which last division a sheriff was appointed, whose duty it was to represent the king in such division, and to see that peace was observed.

Dalton, writing in A.D. 1623, was of opinion that there were sheriffs in this country long before the Saxon invasion, and that the country had been divided into shires prior to the date of their entry into this kingdom; and he gives

Alfred the credit of only rendering the then existing divisions a little more certain and definite; but no proof can be adduced of the existence of such prior divisions—the probability being to the contrary; and the general and best supported opinion is that the credit of parcelling this country into shires or counties is fairly due to Alfred.

Shire is a Saxon word, signifying a *division*, and which comprised an indefinite number of hundreds, while the word County is derived from the Latin *comitatus*, or the *comes* or *count* of the French, or in other words, the *earl* to whom the government of the shire was at first entrusted. The earl, however, by reason of his high position and employment, and his attendance on the king's person (which service in earlier times was required), was not able to transact the business of the county or attend to the duties connected with the office, and was therefore enabled to appoint a deputy, called *vice-comes*, to perform the functions which properly devolved upon himself. This *vice-comes* is the same as the sheriff; and the latter is still called by that name, though he is now quite independent of the earl, the sovereign by letters patent committing to him alone the *custodiam comitatus*. He is considered as Bailiff of the crown, and his county is called his Bailiwick. It would be beyond the province of this dissertation to enumerate the various duties which devolve upon the sheriff, and which are, as Lord Coke says, threefold: "being, 1st, the *vitæ justitiæ*, for no suit begins and no process is served but by the sheriff; secondly, *vitæ legis*, inasmuch as after suits he is chargeable to make execution, which is the life and fruit of the law; and thirdly, *vitæ reipublicæ*, being the *principalis conservator pacis* within the county, which is the life of the commonwealth."

The word Sheriff, according to Impey, Blackstone, and, indeed, most of the legal antiquaries, is derived from the two Saxon words, *scire*, province or shire, or rather from the verb *sciram*, to divide, and *gerefa* or *grave*, the reeve or prefect. Lord Coke says that "shireve" is a word compounded of two Saxon terms, viz., *shire* and *reve satapria* or *comitatus*, and is derived from the Saxon verb *shiram partiri*, for that the whole realm is parted into shires, and *reve* is *præfectus* or *præpositus;* so that "shireve" is the reeve of the shire—*præfectus satapriæ provinciæ seu comitatus.*

Sheriffs were originally chosen by the people in the county court or folk mote, in confirmation of which custom it was enacted by the 28 Ed. I., c. 38, "that the people should have election of their sheriff in every shire, where the shrievalty is not of fee, if they list." The reason of these popular elections, in which appear clear indications of the democratic nature of our early constitution, is given in the same statute, cap. 13: "that the commons might choose such as would not be a burthen to them." However, for the plausible reason that these elections were growing tumultuous, but really because the king wished to have greater authority over the sheriffs, who had now been vested with power to conduct elections of Parliamentary representatives, so that he may be able to have an influence over them in that matter, elections of the sheriffs by the people were put an end to by the 9 Ed. II., c. 2, which ordained —"that the sheriff should from thenceforth be assigned by the chancellor, treasurer, barons of the exchequer, and by the justices, and in the absence of the chancellor, by the treasurer, barons, and justices." By several other statutes, and, finally, by the 21 Hen. VIII., c. 20, it was enacted that "the chancellor, treasurer, president of the king's council, chief justices, and chief baron, are to make this election on the morrow of All Souls in the Exchequer." Since the time of the Sixth Henry it has been the custom for all the Judges, together with the other great Officers of the State, to meet in the Exchequer on the morrow of All Souls annually (which day was altered by a statute of George II. to the morrow of St. Martin), and then and there propose three persons to the sovereign, who afterwards appoints one of them to be sheriff by marking such name with the prick of a pin, and for that reason this particular kind of election is generally called "pricking for sheriffs."

So much of the shrievalty as applicable to England. Now, as Wales formed a distinct kingdom from England at the time of Alfred, and for centuries after him, it is patent to all, that the wise regulations promoted by Alfred did not extend to the Principality, which was governed by its own peculiar laws, compiled, as some say, by Dyvnwal Moelmud, and afterwards augmented and amended by Hywel Dda, under which no division of the country into anything resembling the English shires seems to have been made.

Wales was made subject to English rule in the year 1283, and the first act of the English Legislature affecting the Principality was the *Statutum Walliæ* (12 Ed. I.), passed in the next year, and generally called the Statute of Rhuddlan, the object of which was to render the inhabitants of the Principality subservient to English dominion, and to a great extent to assimilate the laws and administration of justice in Wales to those of England. This statute ordained that there should be sheriffs (therein called *vice-comes*), coroners, and bailiffs of commots in Snowdon and the adjacent parts ; that there should be sheriffs in Anglesea, Caernarvon,

Merioneth, and Flint—the jurisdiction of the last to extend to the City of Chester and to be attendant upon the king's Justiciaries, and to be answerable at the Exchequer of Chester. Sheriffs were also to be appointed for Caermarthen and "*Kardigan ac Lampader cum cantredis, commotis, &c., metis et bundis suis.*" It will be seen by this that at this period several divisions had been meted out even in Wales; but it was not until the reign of Henry VIII. that the existing division of the Principality into shires was effected. The sheriff was by the same statute directed to hold his County Court from month to month and his Tourn twice a year immediately after the Festivals of Easter and St. Michael, and the same jurisdiction was extended to these courts as then prevailed in England.

There is no satisfactory proof that the office of sheriff thus ordained by the *Statutum Walliæ* was afterwards duly recognised, though the late Rev. Charles Henry Hartshorne, in his *History of Caernarvon Castle* (p. 14), alludes to a sheriff of Anglesey in the time of Edward I.

From the date of the above statute until the reign of Henry VIII. the legal polity of Wales did not undergo any important alteration by means of statutory enactment; and it was not until after the accession of Henry VIII. that the entire amalgamation of Wales with England was finally brought about.

No doubt from the date of the subjugation of the Principality by Edward I. the English law generally prevailed; but owing to the tenacity with which the Welsh people adhered to the good old laws framed by Hywel Dda, and the excellent old customs which had been transmitted down from ages past, material differences existed between the laws of the two countries. That English authority might be

maintained and English law disseminated, a Court of the
President and Council was appointed by Royal Commission,
and there were also three justices appointed, viz.—a justice
of Chester, whose jurisdiction included the county of Flint;
a justice of North Wales for the counties of Anglesey,
Caernarvon, and Meirioneth, and a justice of South Wales,
whose jurisdiction extended over the counties of Cardigan,
Pembroke, Caermarthen, and Glamorgan; whilst the rest of
the Principality not having then been divided into counties
as at present, remained subservient to the Lords Marchers—
a most powerful body, enjoying almost regal powers.

Henry VIII. seeing the arbitrary power which was exer-
cised by these Lords Marchers, thought it expedient to the
prosperity of his kingdom, that their dominion should be
curtailed, and the laws of the two countries assimilated.
In the twenty-seventh year of his reign, therefore, an Act
was passed which ordained that the Principality should for
ever thereafter be united to the realm of England, that
persons born therein should enjoy all the privileges of natural
born subjects, and that all the laws, ordinances, and statutes
of England, and none other, should be observed and executed in Wales. That this Act might be fully carried out,
the present division into shires was effected—some of the
baronies of the Lords Marchers being thereby annexed to
certain English counties, and the remainder formed into
new counties under the names of Monmouth, Brecknock,
Radnor, Montgomery, and Denbigh, the first to be considered as an English county, and the others as Welsh
counties. A royal commission was at the same time nominated for the purpose as well as of dividing the counties
thus formed into hundreds, as of settling the divisions of
some others. It was also further enacted that justice should

be administered in these new Welsh counties, and in Caermarthen, Cardigan, Pembroke, and Glamorgan, according to
the English law by such justices as the king should from
time to time appoint, and in such manner as had been used
in the three counties of North Wales, viz.—Anglesey, Caernarvon, and Meirioneth; from which last expression I arrive
at the conclusion that in all probability the *Statutum Wallæ*
of Edward I. was observed to a greater degree in the northern
than in the southern division of the Principality.

The Commission, appointed as above, having reported the
manner in which they had settled the boundaries of the
respective counties and hundreds, another Act of Parliament
was passed in the 34th and 35th years of the same reign, by
which such boundaries were affirmed, and which further
prescribes the mode of judicature to be executed in Wales,
by making provision for the continuance of the President
and Council as theretofore, and enacting that a sessions, to
be called the King's Great Sessions in Wales, should be held
half-yearly in every county, having the same jurisdiction, both
in holding pleas of the Crown and actions-at-law as the
Superior Courts at Westminster. This Sessions has been
now for some time abolished, and assizes are held through-
out Wales in like manner as in England. In addition to
the President and Council and the Justices of Sessions this
Act provided for the creation of Justices of the Peace, and
directed that the Sheriff's County Court should be duly held.

Thus again by statutory enactment the office of sheriff in
Wales was legally recognized, and since the year 1539 sheriffs
have been uninterruptedly appointed for the various counties
of the Principality.

By the same act (c. 26, s. 65) the sheriffs in every of the
shires in Wales were to be nominated by the Lord President

and Council and Justices of Wales, who were to certify the
names to the King's Council, that the King may appoint. By
the 64th section of the Act a fee of five pounds a year was
ordained to be allowed to sheriffs in Wales; such salaries,
however, are not now allowed; and by a recent act (8 & 9
Vic., c. 11) it was provided that Welsh sheriffs should be
nominated and appointed at the same time and place and in
like manner as English sheriffs.

Having thus briefly dwelt on the office of sheriff I shall revert
to the more immediate object of this little work. The fond-
ness of Welshmen for pedigrees is quite proverbial, and like
every thing that is truly Welsh, this passion has been often
sneered at by our neighbours, who, however, would not have
done so had they known its original services. "The Welshman's pedigree was his Title Deed, by which he claimed his
birthright in the country. Everyone was obliged to show his
descent through nine generations in order to be acknowledged
a free native, and by which right he claimed his portion of
land in the community. He was affected with respect to
legal process in his collateral affinities through nine degrees.
For instance, every murder committed had a fine levied on
the relations of the murderer, divided into nine parts, his
brother paying the greatest, and the ninth in affinity the least.
This fine was distributed among the relatives of the victim.
A person passed the ninth descent, formed a new *pen cenedl*,
or head of a family."—*(Meyrick's Cardiganshire.)*

From very ancient times the Welsh therefore paid particular
attention to their pedigrees, and in order to insure the pre-
servation of genuine genealogies the task of registering Arms
and Pedigrees was vested in the *Arwyddveirdd* or Herald
Bards. Originally, it is believed, these heralds were officers
of national appointment; but in the course of time they were

succeeded by the *Prydydd*, or poet the principal duties of whom seem to have been the chronicling of pedigrees. He generally attended the birth, marriage, and death of every man of high descent, and in the *Marwnad* or elegy composed 'upon the decease of such persons, his genealogy was set out from his eight immediate ancestors. A true copy of this was delivered to the heir that it might be placed among the family documents. On the completion of a month from the date of the funeral, the members of the family and their friends used to assemble together in the hall of the mansion, where this copy was produced and then recited in their hearing; and if no error was discovered it was again deposited with the family documents. The bard's fee was a stipend out of every plough land in the district. Besides this he used also to make a triennial circuit,—*clych clerwr,*—for the purpose of arranging pedigrees and making such alterations therein as the change of circumstances required. *(Vide* Introduction to *Dwnn's Heraldic Visitations.)*

Gentility of descent was formerly more esteemed than at present, and necessarily so, for it generally implied good culture; but now that the blessings of education have been to a great extent extended even to the poorer classes in this country, the mere fact of one being possessed of a long pedigree will not ensure respect, nor will the lack of it deprive a man of public esteem if he is endowed with the better qualities of virtue and goodness. Generally speaking an illustrious ancestry has this good effect, that the pride it engenders often deters its possessor from doing any act which might sully the good reputation of his ancestors; but no one should rest his claim to public regard on the length of his pedigree or the good fame of his ancestors, for a glorious ancestry without personal worth is a sham; and Sir Thomas

Overbury truly observed that the "man who has only the excellence of his ancestry to boast of, resembles that edible root, the potato, the best part being under ground."

> "For a' that and a' that,
>   Their dignities and a' that,
> The pith o' sense, and pride o' worth
>   Are higher rank than a' that."

In collecting the materials for this work the author has spared no pains. He has exhausted all the sources at his command, and only regrets that they did not enable him to accomplish his object as he could have wished. He communicated by letter with all those gentlemen now living who served the office, and whose names appear in the list. Some of them proved most ready and willing to assist the author, and rendered valuable assistance by a supply of very interesting matter, for which he feels very grateful.

After the work had gone through the press some further notes were furnished, which are now appended. Should any errors be discovered—and a work of this nature can scarcely be expected to be free of errors—the author will feel obliged to any person who will be kind enough to point them out, so that should future years demand a continuation of the present work, such mistakes may be corrected.

In concluding, the Author begs to convey his especial thanks to Col. Grant Francis, F.S.A., of Cae Bailey, Swansea; the Rev. James Allen, of Castle Martin; and Elliot Lloyd Price, Esq., of Pibwr-wen, Caermarthen, for valuable assistance and interesting communications.

Cilgerran, September 3rd, 1868.

SHERIFFS of CARDIGANSHIRE.

———0———

A LIST of the gentlemen who have served the office of High Sheriff for the County of Cardigan from A.D. 1539, the thirtieth year of the reign of Henry VIII., to A.D. 1867, the thirtieth year of the reign of her present Majesty Queen Victoria.

1539. WILLIAM VAUGHAN, of Cilgerran, co. Pembroke, grandson of Gruffyth Vychan, of Corsygedol, co. Merioneth, a person who rendered very material service to Henry VII. when, as Earl of Richmond, the latter was obliged to quit the country. This William Vaughan was, by a grant of the first year of the reign of Henry VIII., appointed seneschal, receiver, appruator, and forester of Cilgerran, and also constable of the castle during the king's pleasure, whereupon he settled there. He married Margaret, d. of Sir William Perrott, and wore for his *Arms* those of Osborn Fitzgerald, his ancestor, viz., Erm., a saltire, gu. See *Lewys Dwnn's Heraldic Visitations*, vol. 1., pp. 147, 148, and vol. 11., p. 219; and also *Phillips's History of Cilgerran*, p. 106, *et seq.*

1540. SIR JOHN WOGAN, of Wiston, co. Pem., Kt., a lineal descendant, in the male line, of Bleddyn ab Maenarch, last king of Brecknock. This family came to Pembrokeshire on the marriage of Gwgan, son of Bleddyn,

B

with Gwenlliain, heiress of Ffylip Gwys, lord of Wiston. Sir John married Anne (in some pedigrees called Jane), d. and heiress of William Phillips, of Stone Hall, Pembrokeshire, Esq. The *Arms* of Bleddyn were, Sa. a chevron between three spear heads; but according to *Lewys Dwnn* (vol. I., p. 107), Gwgan changed his paternal coat and assumed that of argent, three martlets, or. Sir John was sheriff for Pembrokeshire in 1542. In one pedigree *William* Wogan is stated to have been the sheriff, but such could not be the case, as in all the pedigrees of the family such a name does not appear at this date.

1541. RICHARD HERBERT, of Pencelly, co. Brecknock, Esq. In *Merrick's Cardiganshire*, p. 351, is a pedigree of the Herberts of Havod Uchtryd, where this Richard is surnamed the Black, which is erroneous; as the person who bore the surname was an illegitimate son of William Herbert, Earl of Pembroke, by Maud, d. of one Adam ab William ab Grant, and was the father of William, the first Earl of Pembroke, by fresh creation (*Lewys Dwnn*, vol. I., p. 292); whereas this Richard was the son of Sir Richard Herbert, of Montgomery, by Jane ap William (*ibid*, p. 312). He resided at Pencelly, co. Brecon, and was the father of Richard Herbert, high sheriff for that county in 1597 and 1605 (*Jones's Brecknockshire*, vol. II., pt. 2, p. 592). They were possessed of property in this county, and their *Arms* were, Party per pale sa. and gu. three lions ramp. ar.

1542. SIR THOMAS JONES, of Abermarlaes, co. Caermarthen, Kt., great grandson of Gruffydd ap Nicholas, of Newtown, descended from Urien Reged. Sir Thomas was sheriff for Caermarthenshire in 1541, and married Mary, d. to Sir James Barclay, Kt. (*Dale Castle MSS.*, pub. by Sir Thomas Phillipps, Bart., 1858.)

1543. MORRIS JOHN AB RHYDDERCH, Morfa Bychan, Esq. *Merrick* in his list of Sheriffs calls him Thomas,

which cannot be correct, as there is no such name
in the pedigree of this family—a branch of the powerful family of the lords of Towyn. Morfa Bychan
is situate in the parish of Llanychaiarn, on the sea-
side. Morris was the son of John ab Rhydderch,
of Towyn, by Eliza, d. to Rich. Mortimer, baron of
Coedmawr, and married a d. of Jenkin ab John, of
Deri Caron *(ibid)*.

1544. WILLIAM VAUGHAN, of Cilgerran, Esq. 2nd time.

1545. EDWARD HERBERT, of Montgomery, Esq.

1546. JOHN PHILLIPPS, of Picton Castle, Esq., son of Sir
Thomas Phillipps, Kt., and a lineal descendant of
Cadivor Vawr, lord of Blaencych. He was Sheriff
of Pembrokeshire in 1541, and was twice married
—1stly, to Elizabeth, d. of Sir William Griffiths, of
Anglesey, Chamberlain of North Wales; and, 2ndly,
to Anne, d. of John Voel, of Langridge, Pembrokeshire. The *Arms* of Cadivor, the founder of this
extensive family, were Ar. a lion ramp. guard. sa.;
but the Phillippses, of Picton, bear Ar. a lion ramp.
sa., ducally gorged and chained, or. *Crest*, a lion
ramp. as in arms. *Motto*, Ducit amor patriæ.

EDWARD VI.

1547. RICHARD HERBERT, of Pencelly, Esq. 2nd time. See
1541.

1548. FRANCIS LLOYD, of Hay, co. Montgomery, Esq. This
I presume to be the same as Francis Lloyd, of Great
Haim, Montgomery, whose pedigree is given in the
Her. Vis., vol. 1., p. 289.

1549. WILLIAM HERBERT, of Parcau, co. Montgomery, Esq.,
son of Sir Richard Herbert, of Montgomery, and
brother of the High Sheriff for 1541 and 1547.

1550. DAVID AB JEUAN LLWYD VYCHAN, of Llanvair Clydogau, Esq., descended in a direct male line from
Gwaethvoed Vawr, lord of Ceredigion. He married

Gwenlliain, coheiress of John Gwyn, of Blaen Tren, co. Caermarthen, by whom he had issue. He was again H. S. in 1556 and also in 1569.

1551. Owen Gwyn, of Llanidloes, co. Montgomery, Esq., lineally descended from Gwaethvoed, lord of Powys. A pedigree of this family traced to Adam, the father of Humanity, is given in *Lewys Dwnn's Visitations*, and duly testified by one John Wynne! (Vide vol. i., p. 309.)

1552. Henry Jones, of Newcastle-in-Emlyn, Esq. Probably one of the Abermarlaes family, in whose hands at this period the Castle at this place was.

1553. James Morris, of the town of Cardigan, Esq.

PHILIP AND MARY.

1554. Sir John Wogan, of Wiston, co. Pembroke, Kt. See 1540.

1555. Rhys Vychan ab Rhydderch, of Saint Dogmaels, Esq.

1556. David ab Jeuan Llwyd Vychan, of Llanvair Clydogau, Esq. 2nd time.

1557. David Lloyd ab Robert Vychan, of Beaumaris, co. Anglesey, Esq.

1558. Henry Jones, of Newcastle-in-Emlyn, Esq. 2nd time.

ELIZABETH.

1559. Nicholas Vaughan, of Milton, co. Pembroke, Esq., the fourth husband of Maud Phillipps, d. of Sir Thomas Phillipps, of Picton.

1560. John Vaughan, of Whitland, co. Caermarthen, Esq. (also called Sir John Vaughan, Kt.) He was H. S. for the co. of Pembroke in 1543 and 1555, and for Caermarthenshire in 1552 and 1564.

1561. John Lloyd, of Cilgwyn, Esq., descended from Tudyr Trevor, whose *Arms* this family and that of Gilfachwen bore, viz., Ar. and az. semée of ermine spots ; over all a lion ramp., or, armed and langued gu. According to a pedigree in vol. II. of the *Heraldic Visitation*, p. 34, John Lloyd married a d. of the above John Vaughan, of Whitland, by a d. of Mr. Edmund Catchmey

1562. SIR JOHN WOGAN, of Wiston, grandson of the H. S. for 1540. He married Cecil, d. of Sir Edward Carne, of Ewenny, Kt.

1563. JENKIN GWYN, of Moel Ivor, Esq., a lineal descendant of Cadivor ab Dinawal. He married Lleuku, d. of Hugh ab Gruffydd Jenkin, of Llanddewi Aberarth. Moel Ivor is supposed to be the same as the Llan-rhystid Castle of the Welsh Chronicles. It was pulled down by Jenkin Gwyn during his shrievalty, who erected on its site a large mansion where the present house now stands.

1564. JAMES MORRIS, of Anston, co. Salop, Esq.

1565. HUGH LLEWELLYN LLOYD, of Llanllyr, Esq., the ninth in descent in a direct male line from Cadivor ab Dinawal (*Her. Vis.*, vol. I., p. 52). He married Jane, coheiress of Gruffydd ab Henry. This family bear the *Arms* of Cadivor ab Dinawal, lord of Castell Hywell, viz.: Sa. 3 scaling ladders, and between the two uppermost a spear's head, arg. its point imbrued; on a chief gu. a tripple turreted tower of the second.

1566. RICHARD VAUGHAN, of Whitland, Esq.

1567. JOHN POWELL, of Pen-yr-allt, co. Cardigan, Esq.

1568. JOHN PRICE, of Newtown, co. Montgomery, Esq., a lineal descendant of Tudyr Trevor, through Elytsan Glodrydd. He was the son of Matthew Price, of New-town, by Ioes, a d. of Evan Gwyn, of Mynachty, in whose right he possessed property in this county. He married Elizabeth, d. of Rees ap Maurice, grandson of Evan Blaeney, of Aberbechan, Montgomeryshire; and was grandfather to Sir John Price, who was created a Baronet in 1628. His *Arms* were those of Elystan Godrydd, viz: Quarterly 1st and 4th az. 3 boars' heads, cabossed, sa., langued gu., tusked or; 2nd and

3rd (the coat of Riangor, heiress of Gronwy ab Tudyr Trevor) party per bend sinister, erm. and erminois, over all a lion ramp. or.

1569. DAVID AB JEUAN LLWYD VYCHAN, of Llanvair Clydogau. 3rd time.

1570. GRIFFITH GLYNNE, of Pwllheli, co. Caernarvon, Esq. Probably a member of the Glynne family of Glynllei-von co. Caernarvon, whose pedigree appears in the *Her. Vis.*, vol. II., p. 147.

1571. JAMES LEWIS, of Abernantbychan, Esq. This family is descended from Ednowain ab Bradwen, lord of Llys Bradwen, co. Merioneth, in the 9th century, and who was the founder of the fifteenth noble tribe of North Wales. This James Lewis married Ann, d. of John Wogan, Esq., sheriff in 1562. *Arms*, those of Edno-wain, viz.: Gu. 3 snakes ennowed in a triangular knot, ar.

1572. RHYS DAVID JENKIN, of Aberpylli, Esq. According to his pedigree in the *Her. Vis.*, vol. I., p. 48, he married Gwenlliain, a natural d. of David Lloyd, of Gwernant, but it does not appear that he had any issue by this marriage. He had, however, four natural children, whose names and the names of their mothers are given by Lewys Dwnn, and duly attested by Rhys David Jenkin himself on the 1st day of January, 1588. Rather a curious picture of the state of society during that period! His *Arms* were those of Cadivor ab Dinawal (see under the year 1565), quartering therewith those of Rhys Lloyd, of Creuddyn, and Llewelyn Goch (*ibid*).

1573. THOMAS GRIFFITH, of Maesy-Velin, Esq. Probably the same as is mentioned in the pedigree of Mynydd Hywel, as lord of Lampeter (*Meyrick's Cardiganshire*, p. 211).

1574. MORGAN LLOYD, of Llanllyr, Esq., son of Hugh Llew-ellyn Lloyd, H.S. for 1565. He married Elizabeth, d. and heir of Lewis ab Henry, and was sheriff again in 1583, 1593, and 1598.

1575. JOHN MORTIMER, of Coedmawr, Esq. This family is
supposed to have been derived from Ralph Lord
Mortimer, who accompanied the Conqueror to England. This John was the son of James Mortimer,
Baron of Coedmawr, by Elizabeth, d. of Rhydderch ab
Rhys, lord of Towyn. He married Eve, d. of Lewis
ab Davydd ab Meredydd, of Abernantbychan. A pedigree of the Mortimers appears in the *Her. Vis.*, vol. i.,
p. 34; and the *Arms* borne by this John are stated to
have been, Quarterly, 1st and 4th gu. 2 lions ramp. or,
langued az.; 2nd and 4th gu. a lion ramp. or, within a
bordure indented or.

1576. DAVID LLOYD MEREDYDD, of Cwm Bwn (?), Esq.

1577. JENKIN LLOYD, of Llanvair Clydogau, Esq., son of the
H. S. for 1550. He married Margaret, a d. of John
Stedman, Esq., of Strata Florida, and was a second
time H. S. in 1590.

1578. THOMAS AB RHYS AB WILLIAM, of Ystrad-ffin, co.
Caermarthen, Esq., descended from Cadivor, lord of
Cilycwm, son of Selyv, king of Dyved (*Her. Vis.*, vol. i.,
p. 100). His name appears also on the roll of sheriffs
for the co. of Caermarthen in 1577, 1587, and 1592,
and for the co. of Brecon in 1582. He married Joan,
d. of Sir John ap Rys (Price), of the Priory, Brecon;
of which marriage, I believe, there was no issue.

1579. JOHN PRYSE, of Gogerddan, Esq., lineally descended
from Gwaethvoed Vawr, lord of Cardigan. This family
is one of the most illustrious in the Principality; some
member thereof representing either the county or the
boroughs of Cardigan in almost every parliament since
the time of Queen Elizabeth. This John Pryse married, 1stly, Elizabeth, d. of Sir Thomas Perrott, of
Haroldstone, co. Pembroke, and 2ndly Bridget, d. of
James Pryse, (?) of Mynachty; and by both had issue.
According to the pedigree given in *Meyrick's Cardiganshire*, he was one of the Council of the Marches (p.
397). See also *Her. Vis.*, vol. i., p. 44.

1580. JOHN STEDMAN, of Strata Florida, Esq.; derived according to the pedigree from Galiarbus, duke of Arabia. Jones, in his *History of Brecknockshire*, is rather inclined to doubt the romantic account of the origin of this family (vol. II., pt. I, p. 272.) This John Stedman married Anne, d. of William Phillips, of Pentypare, Esq.; and had issue. The *Arms* of the Stedmans were according to one version a cross fleury vert, in a field or. (*Meyrick's Cardiganshire*, p. 265); but according to Lewys Dwnn, the arms borne by the above High Sheriff were Vert, a cross moline, or (vol. I., p. 88).

1581. THOMAS REVELL, of Forest, co. Pembroke, Esq. He was eldest son of John Revell, of Forest, in the parish of Kilgerran, by Ann, d. of Thomas Walter, one of the Aldermen of Caermarthen, and widow of the celebrated Dr. Thomas Phaer, who translated at Forest into English rhyme the first ten books of *Virgil's Æneid*. According to a pedigree given in the *Her. Vis.*, it appears that the Revell family came into Wales from Shirland Castle, co. Derby, in the time of Edward IV, and settled in Pembrokeshire. The *Arms* of the Revells, of Derbyshire, were Arg. a chevron gu. 3 trefoils ermine, all within a bordure engrailed sa. *Crest*, A bowed arm in armour, garnished, or, holding in the hand a dagger the point downwards, between two bats' wings, or, membraned gu. See *Lewys Dwnn's Visitations*, vol. I., p. 155, *Phillips's History of Cilgerran*, p. 102; and the *General Armoury*. Thomas Revell was also H. S. for co. of Pembroke, in 1579; and again for Cardiganshire, in 1593.

1582. SIR GEORGE DEVEREUX, of Lamphey Court, co. Pembroke, Kt. The family of Devereux were of Norman origin, and derived their surname from a town named Evereux, in Normandy. This gentleman was uncle to the unfortunate Robert Devereux, earl of Essex, at one time the favorite of Queen Elizabeth, who afterwards signed his death warrant. The name of George Devereux appears on the Roll of Sheriffs for the co. of Pembroke, for the year 1580, and for Caermarthenshire for 1581.

1583. MORGAN LLWYD or LLOYD, of Llanllyr, Esq. See 1574.

1584. SIR RICHARD PRYSE, of Gogerddan, Kt., eldest son of the H. S. for 1579, by his first wife. He married Gwenlliain, d. and h. of Thomas Pryse, of Aberbychan, co. Montgomery, by whom he had a numerous issue. He represented the co. of Cardigan in the 7th, 8th, and 10th Parliaments of Elizabeth, and in the 3rd Parliament of James I. He died on the 6th February, 1622, and was buried in the church of Llanbadarn Vawr.

1585 JAMES JONES, of Llanbadarn Vawr, Esq., son of Sir Thomas Jones, of Abermarlaes, by Mary, d. of James Barclay. He married Anne, d. of John Thomas ab Harry, of Crynga, the widow of James ab Lewis ab David Goch, of Llanbadarn. She was the heiress of her brother Richard, and it was in her right that James Jones was possessed of property at Llanbadarn Vawr. See Dolau Cothi Pedigree in *Dale Castle MSS.*, and also *Her. Vis.*, vol. I., p. 62.

1586. SIR GEORGE DEVEREUX, of Lamphey Court. See 1582.

1587. EYNON PHILLIPS, of the Priory, Cardigan, Esq., son of Owen Phillips, of Cilsant, who also by his second wife is the ancestor of the compiler of these sheets. Eynon Phillips married Anne, d. of James Lewes, of Abernantbychan, by whom he had one son, Hector Phillips, father of James and Hector Phillips, who figured so notoriously on the Cromwellian side during the Civil War.

1588. JOHN STEDMAN, of Strata Florida, Esq. See 1580.

1589. JAMES LEWES, of Abernantbychan, Esq. See 1571.

1590. JENKIN LLOYD, of Llanvair Clydogau, Esq. 2nd time.

1591. DAVID LLOYD AB EVAN, of Abermaed, Esq., son of

c

Evan Lloyd, lord of Rhydonen. He married Mary, d. of Watkin Thomas, of Llwyn Iorwerth. This family is deduced by *Lewys Dwnn*, from Edwin ab Goronwy Goch (vol. I., p. 51).

1592. THOMAS REVELL, of Forest, co. Pembroke. 2nd time.

1593. MORGAN LLOYD, of Llanllyr, Esq. See 1574.

1594. JOHN STEDMAN, junior, of Strata Florida, Esq., son of the H. S. for 1580 and 1588. He married Margaret, d. and coh. of David Lloyd ap John. (?)

1595. THOMAS RYS AP WILLIAM, of Ystradffin, co. Caermarthen. 2nd time.

1596. DAVID LLOYD, of Llwyd Jack, Esq., son of Hugh Morgan (deduced from Gwaethvoed Vawr), by Gwenlliain, d. and heiress of John ap Harry, of Tregibby. He married Angharad, d. of John Powel, of Llansawel, and was alive in 1609.

1597. JOHN BIRT, of Llwyndurus, Esq. This family came to Wales from Essex, and first settled at Caermarthen. They bore for *Arms*, Vert, on a chevron gu. 3 bugles ar. between 3 bugles sa., as many trefoils slipped of the first. This John Birt married Anne, d. of Lewis ap Philip, one of the Aldermen of Caermarthen.

1598. MORGAN LLOYD, of Llanllyr, Esq. 4th time.

1599. DAVID LLOYD GWYON, of Llain-vychan, Esq., son of Gwyon, the third son of Llewellyn Lloyd of Castell Hywel.

1600. RICHARD HERBERT, of Pencelli, co. Brecon, Esq., son of the H. S. for 1541. His name appears on the sheriff roll for Brecknockshire for 1597 and 1605.

1601. SIR THOMAS JONES, of Abermarlaes, grandson of the H. S. for 1542. He married Jane, d. and h. of Rowland Pulston, Esq., of Caernarvon, and was sheriff for Caermarthenshire in 1589 and 1603.

1602. JOHN LLOYD, of Llanfair Clydogau, Esq., son of Jenkin Lloyd, H. S. for 1577. He married Jane, d. of Sir Walter Rice, of Newton.

1603. SIR RICHARD PRYSE, of Gogerddan, Kt. 2nd time.

1604. DAVID THOMAS PARRY, of Noyadd-trefawr, Esq. This
family is descended from Rhys Chwith (an esquire of
the body of Edward I.; he bore Sa., a lion ramp. ar.,
armed and langued gu). His descendant, Thomas ap
Harry (whence Parry), of St. Dogmael's, married
Dyddgu, heiress of the Noyadd estate, whose father,
Rhys David Lloyd, was a descendant of Cadwgan, of
Carog, whose *Arms* were those of Cadivor ap Dinawal
(see 1565). David Thomas Parry married and had
issue.

1605. GEORGE PHILLIPS, of the Priory, Cardigan, Esq., son
of the H. S. for 1587.

1606. DAVID LLOYD EVAN, of Abermaed. 2nd time.

1607. JOHN STEDMAN, of Ystrad Fflwr. See 1594. He has
been in several lists described as of Ystradffin, co.
Caermarthen. He was also sheriff for Breconshire in
1609, and is described as of Ystradffin.

1608. SIR JOHN LEWES or LEWIS, of Abernantbychan, Kt., son
of H. S. for 1571. He married Bridget, d. of Sir
Richard Pryse, of Gogerddan (of whom *ante*), and was
the last of the Lewises who resided at Abernantbychan,
which has ever since been the property of the Gogerddan family. (*Meyrick's Cardiganshire*, p. 184.)

1609. THOMAS PRYSE, of Glanffraed, Esq., a brother of the
above Sir Richard Pryse. He married, in 1597, the
heiress of John ap Gruffydd, of Glanffraed.

1610. GEORGE DEVEREUX, of Ystradffin, co. Caermarthen. In
some lists he is called Sir George, and I am inclined to
think him to be the same as the H. S. for 1582. On
the attainder of his nephew, the Earl of Essex, all his
property, save Lamphey Court, was forfeited to the
Crown. The latter property, however, was sold to Sir
Hugh Owen, of Orielton; and, probably, on the sale
the Devereux family removed to Ystradffin.

1611. MORRIS VAUGHAN, of Glanleri, Esq., son of John Vychan, by a d. of Thomas Rhys Lewes, of Llwyn Iorwerth. He married a d. of Griffith Ieuan Jenkin. (*Dale Castle Pedigrees.*)

1612. EVAN GWYN JENKIN, of Moel Ivor, Esq., son of H. S. for 1563.

1613. MORGAN GWYNNE, of Mynachdy. The pedigree of this family in the *Heraldic Visitations* materially differs from that in the *Dale Castle MSS.* According to the former, Morgan Gwynne was the son of Hugh, and married a d. of Morris Gruffydd, of Caernarvonshire, and had issue Lewis, Thomas, and Jane; but the latter states him to have been the son of Lewis Gwynne, to have married the d. of Rhys Gwynne, of Mynachdy, and to have had issue Griffith Gwynne. I cannot ascertain which is correct.

1614. JAMES LEWES, of Cwmowen, Esq. He married the heiress of Edward Morgan, of Glascrug, and became possessed of the estate.

1615. JENKIN DAVID LLOYD GWYNNE (or Gwyon), of Llain-vychan, Esq.; son of H. S. for 1599.

1616. JAMES STEDMAN, of Strata Florida, Esq., son of the H. S. for 1594. He died while in office, and was succeeded by

DAVID THOMAS PARRY, of Noyadd, Esq., of whom see 1604.

1617. THOMAS JONES, of Llanbadarn-vawr, Esq., son of the H. S. for 1585. He was twice married, and bore for *Arms* those of Urien Rheged.

1618. EDWARD VAUGHAN, of Trawsgoed (Crosswood), Esq., son of Jenkin Vaughan. He married Lettice, d. of John Stedman, of Strata Florida, and had issue John Vaughan, who afterwards became the celebrated Sir John Vaughan, Kt., Lord Chief Justice of the Common Pleas, and of whom the following character is given in an old MS., written about 1661, entitled "A true character of the deportment for these 18

yeares last past of the principal gentry within the
counties of Caermarthen, Pembroke, and Cardigan,
in South Wales."

"John Vaughan, one that will upon fitts talk loud for mon-
archy; but scrupulous to wet his finger to advance it. He served
burgess for Cardigan in the Long Parliament, but quitted it
upon Strafford's tryal; named by His Majesty one of the Com-
missioners to attend the treaty in the Isle of Wight, but refused
it; personally advized Cromwell to put the crowne on his own
head, purchased Mevenyth, one of his late Majesty's manors within the county of Cardigan; personally assisted in the taking of
Aberystwith, a garrison then kept for his late Majesty. These
services kept him from sequestration; bore offices in the late
several Governments. He is of good parts; but putts to high
a value on them; insolently proud and matchlessly pernicious;
by lending eight hundred pounds to Colonel Philip Jones, and
other favourites of the late tymes, procured the command of the
county he liveth in to continue his friends, and dependent to this
day."

An engraving of this personage is given in *Yorke's
Royal Tribes of Wales.* He twice represented the Borough, firstly in 1640, a parliament of only twenty-
one days' duration, and secondly in the Long Parliament, which lasted sixteen years, eight months, and
sixteen days. He was disabled in 1645, but again
re-instated.

1619. DAVID LLOYD EVAN, of Abermaed, Esq. See 1591.
1620. JOHN PARRY, of Blaenpant, Esq., a member of the
Noyadd family. Dying while in office, he was succeeded by
DAVID THOMAS PARRY, Esq., Sheriff for the 3rd time.
1621. WALTER LLOYD, of Llanvair Clydogau, Esq., son of
H. S. for 1602. He was afterwards knighted.
1622. EVAN GWYNNE JENKIN, of Moel Ivor. 2nd time.
1623. JOHN PRYSE, of Strata Florida, Esq. He married the
widow of the H. S. for 1616, and came to reside at
Strata Florida.
1624. EVAN LLOYD GWYN, of Llandissil-uwch-Cerdin, Esq.

CHARLES I.

1625. THOMAS PRYSE, of Ynysgerigog, Esq., son of H. S. for 1609.

1626. SIR HENRY JONES, Abermarlaes, Kt. In the pedigree he is styled Baronet. Son of Sir Thos. Jones (see 1601), and married a d. of Richard Herbert, of Montgomery.

1627. LLEWELLYN THOMAS PARRY, of Tyglyn, Esq.

1628. JOHN PUGH, of Glanffraed, Esq.

1629. JAMES LEWES, of Cwm Owen, Esq. (2nd time). Dying while in office, the vacancy was filled by

STEPHEN PARRY, of Cwm-tydu, Esq., one of the Parrys of St. Dogmael's, who obtained Cwmtydu through marrying the heiress of Thomas Gwyn, of that place.

1630. DAVID PARRY, of Noyadd-trefawr, Esq.

1631. ROWLAND PUGH, of Mathavarn, co. Montgomery, Esq. This was one of the principal families in Montgomeryshire from the 15th to the 18th centuries, and is traced in a direct line to Seisyllt, lord of Merioneth. Several members of this family have been sitting in Parliament, and, among others, this gentleman represented the Borough of Cardigan in the first Parliament of Charles I., in 1625. This family became connected with the county of Cardigan through marriages into the families of Glanffraed, Gogerddan, and Coedmawr. Rowland Pugh had for his first wife Elizabeth, second d. of Sir Richard Pryse, of Gogerddan, and for his second wife Mary, d. of James Lewes, of Coedmawr, by both of whom he had issue. By his second wife, he was grandfather to William Pugh, barrister-at-law, M.P. for Montgomeryshire, and who was alive in 1711 (*Her. Vis.*, vol. I., pp. 295, 296). The Mathavarn estate was sold in 1752 to an ancestor of the present Sir Watkin W. Wynne, Bart., M.P. Of one member of the Pugh family the following stanza says :

"Oh, Mr. Pughe ! y chwi yw'r pen,
Mathavarn wen sydd enwog ;
Parch a succour yr holl sir,
Ac arglwydd tir Cyveiliog."

1632. RHYS LLOYD, of Bronwydd, Esq. He was son of the
Rev. Thomas Lloyd, rector of Llangunllo, and married a d. of John Parry, of Blaenpant. He is an
ancestor of the present Sir Thomas Davies Lloyd, of
Bronwydd, Bart., M. P.

1633. SIR JOHN LEWES, of Abernantbychan, Kt,   See 1608.

1634. HECTOR PHILLIPS, of Tregibby, Esq. Son of George
Phillips, H. S. in 1605. He and his brother James
Phillips, of the Priory, (who sat in Parliament during
the Commonwealth for this County) were famous
sequestrators during the infamous civil war, and obtained for themselves an unenviable notoriety. According to the pedigree of this family he married, 1st, Mary,
d. of Philip Scippon, governor (?) of London ; and
2ndly, Margaret, d. of Richard Owen, of Rhiwsaeson, in
Montgomery, and widow of James Stedman, of Glandovan and Strata Florida,   Hector Phillips was Mayor
of Cardigan in 1657, 1666, and 1678.

1635. JOHN LEWES, of Cwm Owen, Esq., son of James Lewes,
H. S. for 1629. He married Mandeline, d. and
h. of Rhys, third son of Morgan David Lloyd, of
Glascrug, and had issue one son.

1636. THOMAS PRYSE, of Ynysgerigog.   2nd time.

1637. JOHN STEDMAN, of Strata Florida, Esq., son of H. S. for
1616, and married Jane, d. of Edward Vaughan, of
Trawsgoed (see 1618), by whom he had issue James
Stedman, afterwards of Glandovan, Cilgerran.

1638. JOHN LLOYD, of Crynfryn, Esq.

1639. RICHARD PRYSE, of Gogerddan, Esq., grandson of Sir
Richard Pryse, Kt., being a son of Sir Richard's eldest
son, Sir John Pryse, of Aberbychan, co. Montgomery,
by Mary, d. of Sir Henry Bromley, of Shraddon Castle,
co. Salop. This Richard Pryse married, 1st, Hester, d.

of Sir Hugh Middleton, Bart., and had issue by her three sons; 2ndly, Mary, d. of Lord Ruthin. He represented this co. from 1640 to 1653, and was created a baronet on the 9th August, 1641.

1640. JENKIN DAVID LLOYD GWYNNE, of Llainvychan, Esq 2nd time.

1641. DAVID EVANS, of Llechwedd-dery, Esq.

1642. HENRY VAUGHAN, of Cilcenin, Esq. Of him the following character is given in the MS. before alluded to (see 1618):—

"Harry Vaughan, anything for money, a proselyte and favorite to all the changes of tymes; a sheriff for his late Majesty, afterwards for Cromwell; justice of the peace under each, tyrant in power, mischievous by deceit; his motto---Qui nescit dissimulare, nescit vivere."

1643. THOMAS LLOYD, of Danyfforest, Esq. He was third son of Sir Walter Lloyd, of Llanvair-Clydogau, and married Jane, d. of Sir Marmaduke Lloyd, of Maesyvelin, by whom he had only one daughter, who afterwards married Thomas Johnes, Esq., heir of Dolau Cothi.

1644. THOMAS LLOYD continued in office two years.

KING AND PARLIAMENT.

1645. JAMES LEWES, of Cilcyffeth, co. Pembroke, Esq.

1646. JAMES LEWES, of Cwm Owen, Esq. (? John).

1647. THOMAS LLOYD, of Llanllyr, Esq. He married Lettice, d. of Sir John Pryse, of Gogerddan.

THE KEEPERS OF THE LIBERTIES OF ENGLAND.

1648. HUGH LLOYD, of Lloyd Jack, Esq. He is, I think, the one who married the d. of David Lloyd, of Alltyrodyn.

1649. JAMES PHILLIPS, of Tregibby, Esq., the eldest brother of the H. S. for 1634. He was thrice married, 1st, to Frances, d. of Sir Richard Phillips, of Picton, Bart.; 2ndly, to Catherine, d. of John Fowler, of London, Esq. This lady is popularly known as the "Matchless

Orinda," and was a poetess of acknowledged genius. A book of Poems, written by her, was printed in 1658; and subsequent to her decease an account of her life was published. She left behind her one daughter, who married Lewis Wogan, of Bolton, Esq. James Phillips's third wife was Anne, d. of Sir Richard Rudd, of Aberglasney, Bart. He was one of those who represented Wales in Cromwell's Little Parliament, summoned in 1653, to which no representatives from any cities or boroughs were summoned except London, and only a few returned for counties in general. In the second Parliament of Cromwell, convened on the 3rd September, 1654, and dissolved the 22nd of the following January, he represented the county of Cardigan, as did he also in the third Parliament, which assembled on the 26th June, 1657, and which was a very shortlived one. Between 1646 and 1653, he advocated the claim of the inhabitants of Cardigan to have a free school in the town; and, from unpublished documents in my possession, was so far successful as to obtain, in 1653, a lease of the sequestrated livings of Llansaintffraed and Lampeter towards the maintenance and support of such a school. The school thus founded is now, and has ever since been, in existence at Cardigan, though its original endowment was on the Restoration justly taken away and restored to the clergymen, from whom it had been sequestrated. Of him the following character appears in the old MS. before mentioned :—

" James Phillips, one that had the fortune to be in with all tymes, yet thrived by none, an argument that covetousness (the root of all evil) was not the motive for him to take employments; his genius is to undertake publique affayres, regarding some tymes more the employment than the authority from whom he received the same. He hath done much good, and is ill rewarded by those he deserved most of."

1650. JOHN LLOYD, of Vairdrev, Esq., son of Jenkin Lloyd, of Vairdrev, a descendant of Rhydderch ab Tydyr. He

D

married a d. of Morgan Herbert, of Havod-Ychtryd. This gentleman was the last of the Lloyds, of Vairdrev. Dying without issue, the estate devolved upon his father's sister, who had married into the Llanerch-aeron family; and in whose possession it still remains.

1651. RICHARD EVAN LLOYD, of Ystrad-teilo, son of Evan Lloyd ab John, of Llanbadarn-vawr, a lineal descendant in the male line of Elystan Glodrydd, lord of Fferllys and founder of the fourth Royal Tribe of Wales. The *Arms* of this family were, Quarterly 1st and 4th. Gu. a lion ramp. reguard. or.; 2nd and 3rd arg. 3 boars' heads, couped sa. *(Meyrick's Cardiganshire, p. 301.)*

1652. THOMAS PARRY, of Towyn, Esq.

OLIVER CROMWELL, LORD PROTECTOR.

1653. THOMAS EVANS, of Peterwell, Esq., eldest son of the High Sheriff for 1641. He married a d. of Evan Gwynne, of Moel Ivor. Of him the following character is given in the MS. I have so often quoted :—

> "Thomas Evans, passionately violent in anything; first a covenanter, than an eager advocate for the negative oath; afterwards most impetuous against a single person, especially the family of his now Majestie; an active Captain of Horse, and his son, David, of Foote, under the late Committee of Safety; passing an oath upon others for their fidelity to the said committee; endeavouring to incite men, about the beginning of April last, to take arms against General Monke; impatient without an office, and tyrannical in it."

1654. HENRY VAUGHAN, of Cilcenin, Esq. See 1642.

1655. SIR RICHARD PRYSE, of Gogerddan, Bart. 2nd time. See 1639.

1656. THOMAS LLOYD, of Llanvair Clydogau, Esq. 3rd time.

1657. MORGAN HERBERT, of Havod Ychtryd, Esq. The Herbert family, of Havod Ychtryd, was a branch of the Montgomeryshire family, and claim descent from Henry I., king of England. This Morgan Herbert was, as will appear, High Sheriff for four consecutive years, under four different governments. He died in 1687, leaving issue William Herbert, of the same place, who died in 1704. *Arms*, Party per pale sa. and gu., three lions ramp. arg.

1658. MORGAN HERBERT, of Havod Ychtryd, Esq.

1659. MORGAN HERBERT, of Havod Ychtryd, Esq.

1660. MORGAN HERBERT, of Havod Ychtryd, Esq. 4th time.

1661. THOMAS LLOYD, of Rhiwarthen, Esq.

1662. DAVID LLOYD, of Crynvryn, Esq., eldest son of H. S. for 1638,

1663. WATKIN LLOYD, of Wern-newydd, Esq., grandson of Dd. Lloyd of the same place, the 4th son of David Lloyd Gruffydd, of Vairdref.

1664. JAMES LEWES, junior, of Coedmawr, Esq., son of James Lewes, by a d. of John Wogan, of Wiston, and grandson of Sir John Lewes, who exchanged Castell Llwyd with Rowland Mortimer for Coedmawr. He was a colonel in King James's army, and married a d. of Col. Richard Harrison, of Hurst, Berks, by whom he had a son, John Lewes, who was H. S. for Brecknockshire in 1684, possessing property there in right of his wife, the d. of Lodwick Lewis, of Llangors. The character of Col. James Lewis is thus given in the ancient MS. before alluded to :—

> "James Lewes is a person of an inoffensive, facile constitution, forced from a Royalist to act as a colonel for king and parliament; seldom out of publique offices, though averse to undertake any; loved more for doing no wrong than for doing of any good. *Sola socordia innocens.*"

1665 JOHN JONES, of Nanteos, Esq., second son of Edwar.'

Jones by Margaret, d. of James Lewes, of Abernantbychan. He was a colonel of a Foot Regiment raised
in this county for the service of King Charles I., " of
blessed memory ;" and married Mary, d. of Jasper
Cornelius. He is thus noticed in the aforesaid MS.:—

> " John Jones, one that appeared in the first publique differ-
> ences for monarchy, and much suffered by reason thereof ; yet, in
> 1647, he assisted the reducing of Aberystwith, a garrison then
> holden for the king, it was thought upon a personall injury offered
> him ; his principles being stedfastly fixed for monarchy, and the
> true heir thereof ; for he was constantly imprisoned, on all securing
> payd a deepe fine in Goldsmith's Hall, decimated and grievously
> sequestered, declyned, though sometimes tendred publique offices
> whatsoever ; the constant object of the phanatique hatred ; but
> one of mean parts, only wise in that he is partly sensible of the
> meanness of them."

A very different version of his character is given
on a monument at Llanbadarnvawr Church, where he
was buried, by which it appears that

> " He was true to the church in time of persecution, to the
> king in time of rebellion, when, for doing good, he suffered
> much evil."

By his marriage he had three daughters, of whom
see pedigree in *Meyrick's Cardiganshire.*, p. 402.

1666. JOHN WILLIAMS (?), of Abernantbychan, Esq.

1667. JAMES STEDMAN, of Glandovan, Esq., son of the H. S.
for 1637.

1668. DAVID LLOYD, of Alltyrodyn, Esq. Descended from
the ancient family of Castell Hywel. This David
Lloyd married Mary, d. of Henry Pryse of Abergor-
lech, by whom he had a numerous issue. He was,
like most of the Welsh gentry, a warm Royalist, and
during the ascendancy of the revolutionary party, he
was, in 1638, declared a delinquent, and his property
sequestered ; for which his son afterwards compounded. *(Meyrick's Cardiganshire.)*

1669. WILLIAM SUMMERS, of Llanllyr, Esq.

1670. HECTOR PHILLIPS, of Tregibby, Esq., grandson of the
H. S. for 1587. He and his brother, James Phillips,
of the Priory, Cardigan, played a conspicuous part
during the Civil War, and were notorious and unprin-
cipled sequestrators. As it is the author's intention
some day to publish a detailed history of the Civil
War in Wales, the characters of these men must be
left until that occasion.

1671. JAMES JOHNES, of Abermaed, Esq., son of the H. S.
for 1617. He was twice married, and by his second
wife, a d. of John Pryse, of Gogerddan, had issue one
son, who inherited the Abermaed estate.

1672. JOHN LEWES, junior, of Gernos, Esq. He married
Margaret, d. of Walter Jones, of Llwynfortyn, by
whom he had only one d., who was married to Thos.
Parry of Cwmeynon.

1673. HUGH LLWYD, of Llwydgoch, Esq.

1674. THOMAS JOHNES, of Llanvair Clydogau, Esq. He was
of Dolau Cothi, and possessed Llanvair Clydogau in
right of his wife, Elizabeth, heiress of Thomas Lloyd,
of that place.

1675. NICHOLAS LEWES, of Pantyrodyn, Esq., son of Richard
Lewes, of Gernos. He married a d. of Morris Morgan,
of Coedllwyd, Clydau, co. Pem.

1676. CORNELIUS LE BRUN, of Nanteos, Esq. A native of
Cologne, who married Anne, second d. of Col. John
Jones, in whose right (the heiress having died without
issue) he enjoyed the estate. He was naturalized in
1663, and, dying in 1703, was buried at Llanbadarn-
fawr, where a monument was put up to his memory.

1677. MORGAN LLWYD, of Green Grove, Esq.

1678. JOHN PHILLIPS, of Dolhaidd, Esq., son of John Phillips,
of the same place, by Mary, d. of John Lewes, of
Glascrug. Her brother, James Lewes, dying without
issue, she became entitled to those estates, in right
whereof her son served the office of Sheriff.

1679. EDWARD JONES, of Llanina, Esq., a descendant of

Cadwgan Grach, of Carog.   He became possessed of
the estate under the will of his half-brother, Daniel
Gwynne, of the Moel Ivor family ; not, however, before
the will had been contested. *(Merrick's Card.,* p. 238.)

1680.   THOMAS LLOYD or LLWYD, of Bronwydd, grandson of
H. S. for 1632. He married Bridget, d. of James
Jones, of Dolau Cothi, co. Caermarthen.

1681.   THOMAS PRYSE, of Ynysgerigog, Esq., son of H. S.
for 1636.

1682.   MORGAN LLOYD, of Ffoshelig, Esq., son of Hugh
Lloyd, by Ann, d. of George Lloyd, of Castell Hywel.

1683.   JOHN LLOYD, of Cilgwyn, Esq.

1684.   JOHN HERBERT, of Gogerddan, Esq.

JAMES II.

1685.   DAVID PARRY, of Noyadd-trefawr, Esq., son of H. S.
for 1630.

1686.   EVAN LLOYD, of Alltyrodyn, Esq.

1687.   HUGH POWELL, of Nantgwyllt, co. Radnor, Esq.

1688.   HECTOR PHILLIPS, of The Priory, Cardigan, Esq.
2nd time.

WILLIAM III. AND MARY.

1689.   WILLIAM HERBERT, of Havod Ychtryd, Esq., son of
H. S. for 1657. He died in 1704, leaving an only
daughter, who married Thomas Johnes, of Llanvair
Clydogau.

1690.   SIR CHARLES LLOYD, of Maesyvelin, Kt., a natural son
of Sir Francis Lloyd, by Bridget Leigh, his concubine.

1691.   RICHARD LLOYD, of Mabws, Esq.

1692.   DANIEL EVANS, of Peterwell, Esq., son of Thomas
Evans and grandson of David Evans, of Llechwedd-
dery, one of Cromwell's agents, who is said to have
enriched himself on the spoils of the church, and of
the Royalists.

1693. RICHARD STEDMAN, of Strata Florida, Esq., son of the
     H. S. for 1667.

1694. DAVID LLOYD, of Crynvryn, Esq.

1695. FRANCIS VAUGHAN, of Glanlery, Esq.

1696. VAUGHAN PRYSE, of Cilcenin, Esq.,—since made Bart.

1697. HUGH LLOYD, of Lloyd Jack, Esq.

1698. JOHN KNOLLES, of Ynyshir, Esq. He was Mayor of
     Cardigan for the year 1693.

1699. RODERICK RICHARDES, of Aberystwith, Esq., the son
     of Richard Rhydderch, of the same place. It was he
     who built Penglais, now in the possession of a descen-
     dant of his.

1700. JOHN PHILLIPS, of Cwm Owen, and also of Dolhaidd,
     co. Caermarthen, Esq.

1701. RICHARD LEWIS, of Cefn Gwyn or Alltfadog, Esq.

QUEEN ANNE.

1702. LEWIS GWYNNE, of Mynachty, Esq., grandson of the
     Sheriff for 1613. He married Mary, d. of John Pryse,
     of Rhandir, Esq., by whom he had four sons and
     two daughters.

1703. RICHARD PHILLIPS, of Moel Ivor, brother of H. S. for
     1700.

1704. MORGAN HOWELLS, of Penybaily, Esq.

1705. THOMAS JOHNES, of Llanvair Clydogau, Esq., son of
     H. S. for 1674. He married Anne, d. of Dd. Lloyd,
     of Crynfryn.

1706. JOHN LLOYD, of Peterwell, Esq.

1707. THOMAS LLOYD, of Bronwydd, Esq. He married Anne,
     d. of Lewis Wogan, of Wiston.

1708. NATHANIEL GRIFFITHS, of Mountain Hall, co. Carnar-
     von, Esq.

1709. JOHN JOHNES, of Abermaed, Esq., son of H. S. for
     1671, by his second wife.

1710. DAVID LLOYD, of Llanvechan, Esq.

1711. JOHN LEWIS, of Gernos, Esq.

1712. REES DAVID MORRIS, of Blaendyffryn, Esq.

1713. MORGAN LLOYD, of Abertrinant, Esq.

1714. HUGH LLOYD, of Aberllolwyn, Esq.

GEORGE I.

1715. JOHN JONES, of Rhosgellan, Esq.

1716. THOMAS HUGHES, of Hendre Velen, Esq. He was one
of the early patrons of Mr. Edward Richards, the
founder of the excellent Grammar School, at Ystrad-
meirig.

1717. RICHARD MORRIS, of Carog, Esq.

1718. DAVID LLOYD, of Lloyd Jack, Esq., son of the High
Sheriff for 1697.

1719. THOMAS KNOLLES or KNOWLES, of Wenallt, Esq. He
served the office of Mayor of the Borough of Cardigan during the year 1713.

1720. STEPHEN PARRY, of Rhydymendi, Esq. He was the
eldest son of David Parry, of Noyadd-trefawr, H. S.
for 1685, and was elected a Member of Parliament for
the county of Cardigan, in 1721. He died without
issue in 1724, and was buried at Llandugwydd, where
a monument has been erected to his memory.

1721. EDWARD LLOYD, of Wern-newydd, Esq., son of Dd.
Lloyd, of the same place. He died in London and
was interred in Audley Chapel, Grosvenor Square, in
the year 1754.

1722. WALTER LLOYD, of Coedmawr, Esq., son of John
Lloyd, of Coedmawr, by Miss Lloyd, of Mabws. He
married Anna Posthuma Thomas, of the co. of Caermarthen, by whom he had one son and two daughters.
The Lloyd family of Coedmawr and Cilgwyn are a
branch of the Gilfachwen family, and trace their
descent directly from Elystan Glodrydd, Prince of
Fferllys and Lord of Builth, founder of the fourth
Royal Tribe of Wales, who bore for *Arms* gu. a lion
ramp. regard. sa.

1723. JAMES GRIFFITH, of Noyadd, Llanarth, Esq. He married a d. of Watkin Lloyd, of Wern-newydd, and left only one d., who married Col. Brooks.

1724. DAVID JONES, of Penyrallt, Llangoedmore, Esq. He was again Sheriff in 1748, and died in the year 1763, and was buried at Llangoedmore.

1725. WILLIAM WILLIAMS, of Ddolgoch, Esq.

1726. DAVID LEWIS, of Gernos, Esq.

1727. LEWIS LEWIS, of Cefn Gwyn, Esq., son of H.S. for 1701.

GEORGE II.

1728. JOHN JONES, of Ty'rglyn or Tyglyn Isaf, Esq.

1729. EDWARD JONES, of Llanina, Esq. The Llanina estate came into the possession of the Jones family, under the will of Daniel Gwynne, of Moel Ivor, which was contested by the Gwynnes in the reign of Charles II., but was decided in favour of the Joneses. (*Vide Meyrick's Cardiganshire.*)

1730. JOHN LEWIS, of Caermarthen, Esq.

1731. JOHN LLOYD, of Cilgwyn, Esq.

1732. JOHN PRICE, of Blaendyffryn, Esq.

1733. THOMAS LLOYD, of Bronwydd, Esq., eldest son of H.S. for 1707. He married Anne, d. of William Lloyd, of Henllys and Penpedwast, who was the heir general of the Owens, of Henllys, and through whom the Lordship Marcher of the Barony of Kemes came into the Bronwydd family.

1734. DAVID JONES, of Tyglyn-isaf, Esq., son of H.S. for 1728.

1735. W. O. BRIGSTOCKE, of Blaenpant, Esq.

1763. ROBERT DYER, of Llangathen, co. Caermarthen, Esq. He married Frances, youngest d. of Sir Herbert Croft, Bart., M.P. for the co. of Hereford. (*Vide Burke's Landed Gentry.*)

1737. THOMAS JOHNES, of Abermaed, Esq. A member of the Johnes' family, of Llanbadarn, for whose pedigree see *Meyrick's Cardiganshire*, p. 359.

E.

1738. FRANCIS INGRAM, of Glanleri, Esq.

1739. JOHN PHILIPPS, of Cryngae, Esq.

1740. THOMAS JOHNES, of Llanio, Esq. He died while in office.

1741. THOMAS LEWIS, of Llwyngrawys, Esq. This gentleman was a member of the Abernantbychan family, and an ancestor of the present Major William Henry Lewis, of Clynfiew, co. Pembroke, whose *Arms* are those of Ednowain ab Bradwen, viz., gu. three snakes ennowed in a triangular knot, arg.

1742. DANIEL BOWEN, of Waen-Ivor, Esq.

1743. DANIEL LLOYD, of Alltyrodyn, Esq., great-grandson of H.S. for 1668. He married Justina, d. of John Price, of Blaendyffryn.

1744. CHARLES GWYNNE, of Mynachdy, Esq., fourth son of H.S. for 1702. His three elder brothers having died without issue, he succeeded to the property, and married Bridget, d. of John Jones, of Tyglyn, by whom he had five children, all of whom, however, died without issue, and the property was devised by Charles's eldest son, Lewis, who died in 1805, to the Rev. Alban Thomas (who took the name of Jones on his marriage with his cousin, Susannah Maria Jones, of Tyglyn, who was also cousin to the said Lewis Gwynne). The *Arms* of the Gwynne family are, Azure, three stags' heads, in fess a mullet; some say, cross crosslet.

1745. DAVID PARRY, of Noyadd-trefawr, Esq., grandson of H.S. for 1685, being the son of William Parry, of Nevern.

1746. SIR LUCIUS CHRISTOPHER CORNWALLIS LLOYD, of Maesyvelin, son of Sir Charles Lloyd, by a d. of Sir Francis Cornwallis, of Abermarlaes, co. Caermarthen. He married Anne, d. of Walter Lloyd, of Peterwell, and dying without issue, he left his estate to his brother-in-law, John Lloyd.

1747. WILLIAM LEWIS, of Lanlas, Esq. (?)

1748. DAVID JONES, of Penyrallt, Esq. Second time.

1749. LEWIS PRYSE, of Abernantbychan, Esq. A member of the Gogerddan family, into whose hands the estate of Abernantbychan fell after the death of Sir John Lewis, who had married a d. of Sir Richard Pryse.

1750. JOHN MORGAN, of Cardigan, Esq. He married a d. of Sir Francis Cornwallis, of Abermarlaes, and died in 1763. A monument was erected to his memory, and stands in the churchyard of St. Mary, Cardigan.

1751. WILLIAM WILLIAMS, of Pantyseiri or Pantysheriff, Esq., son of H.S. for 1725, and grandson of John Williams, of Llanddewibrevi, gent., by Johan Price. He was a man of great ability and influence. He made large sums of money by breeding sheep. Occasionally his stock of sheep amounted to 19,000, but never reached 20,000; and in the obituary in the *Gentleman's Magazine* at the time of his death, he is stated to have been known as the "King of the Mountains."

1752. JOHN LEWES, of Llanllyr, Esq.

1753. LEWIS ROGERS, of Gelli, Esq.

1754. JOHN EDWARDS, of Abermeirig, Esq.

1755. WILLIAM BOWEN, of Troedyraur, Esq., son of John Bowen, of the same place, whose grandfather changed the name of Owen into that now in use by the family. William Bowen married Rebecca, eldest d. and co-h. of Mr. Willy, of Whitehouse, co. Pembroke, and had issue three sons and four daughters, all of whom died without issue. *Arms*, gu. a lion ramp. regard. or: *Crest*, a nag's head bridled.

1756. LEWIS LLOYD, of Gernos, Esq.

1757. JOHN GRIFFITHS, of Penpontbren, Esq.

1758. ABEL GRIFFITHS, of Pantybettws, Esq.

1759. GEORGE PRICE, of Rhydcolomenod, Esq.

1760. THOMAS HUGHES, of Hendre Velen, Esq., son of H.S. for 1716.

GEORGE III.

1761. WALTER LLOYD, of Coedmawr, Esq.

1762. DAVID LLOYD, of Brynog, Esq.

1763. JOHN PAYNTER, of Havod Ychtryd, Esq. He took a
lease for his life of Havod from Mr. Johnes, and some
letters of his to the then Bishop of St. David's respect-
ing the church of Eglwys Newydd are preserved in
Meyrick's Cardiganshire, p. 362, &c.

1764. THOMAS JONES, of Noyadd, Esq.

1765. THOMAS EVANS, of Blaengwenog, Esq.

1766. WILLIAM JONES, of Dolyclettwr, Esq.

1767. RICHARD MORGAN, of Llysvaen, Esq.

1768. DANIEL LLOYD, of Laques, co. Caermarthen, Esq. This
family traces its descent from Blegwrech ab Dinawal.
Daniel Lloyd was a barrister-at-law, and was the son
of William Lloyd, of Laques, by his third wife, Jane,
d. of John Davies, of Dolaugwynion, co. Cardigan.

1769. JOHN HUGHES, of Tymawr, Esq.

1770. RODERICK RICHARDES, of Pen-y-glais, Esq., son of
Richard Rhydderch. It was he who built the mansion
house at Penyglais.

1771. LEWIS GWYNNE, of Mynachty, Esq., son of H.S. for
1744. He died in 1805, and left his property to the
Rev. Alban Thomas and his wife (who was the cousin
of the said Lewis Gwynne) for their lives, with remainder to their only son, the late A. T. J. Gwynne, Esq.

1772. LLEWELLYN PARRY, of Gernos, Esq.; a descendant of
Davydd ab Ieuan, of Llwyndavydd, co. Cardigan.
This Davydd entertained Henry, Earl of Richmond,
at Llwyndavydd on his expedition against Richard III.,
and for which he received various presents from Henry
when he became King of England; and among others
a beautiful drinking horn, which is now preserved at
Golden Grove, and is the property of the Earl of
Cawdor. An engraving of this horn forms the frontis-
piece to the Welsh MS. Society's edition of *Lewys
Dwnn's Heraldic Visitations*. Llewellyn Parry was the
grandson of Thomas Parry, of Cwmcynon, who married the heiress of John Lewis, of Gernos. He bore

for his *Arms*, quarterly 1st. sa. a lion ramp. arg.; 2nd, arg. 3 **boars'** heads, couped, sa.; 3rd, gu. a lion ramp. regard. **or**; and 4th, gu. 3 snakes entwined proper, **arg.**

1773. **JOHN** JONES, of **Deri** Ormond, Esq. This ancient family **removed** from Denbighshire into the **co. of** Cardigan **about** the year 1672, and are descended in a direct **line** from Ednowain Bendew, founder **of one** of the Noble Tribes **of North Wales**, whose *Arms* the present representative **of the family** now bears: viz., Arg. a **chevron between 3 boars' heads** couped sa. This **Mr.** Jones **married in** 1770 Miss Hannah Smith, of Eustone House, **near London, by** whom he had issue **two sons and four daughters, viz.,** John Jones, who **succeeded** him, and of whom see 1818; **Richard Jones, who died** while **at Cambridge;** Hannah, m. Rhys **Powell, Esq., of Craig-y-nôs, co. Brecknock;** Elizabeth, m. the Rev. **Richard Board, of Board Hill** and **Pax** Hill **Place, Sussex,** rector of Westerham, Kent.; Catherine, m. **Sir Astley Paston** Cooper, **of Gadesbridge Park, co. Hertford, Bart.;** and Henrietta, m. James **Paterson, of Stirling,** and Cornwall Terrace, **Regent's Park, Esq., eldest son of General** Paterson, Royal **Artillery, and great-grandson of Bishop** Paterson.

1774. THOMAS **LLOYD, of Abertrinant,** Esq.

1775. EDWARD VAUGHAN, of Green Grove, **Esq.**

1776. NATHANIEL **WILLIAMS**, of Pant-y-Sheriff, Esq., second son of **the H.S. for** 1725, **and** brother **of the** H.S. for 1751. He married Elizabeth, d. **of John** Jones, **of** Diserth, **co.** Radnor, and died in **1793,** leaving issue one son and three daughters.

1777. DAVID EDWARD **LEWES** LLOYD, **of** Dolhaidd, Esq.

1778. THOMAS BOWEN, **of** Waen Ivor, **Esq.,** son of H.S. for 1742.

1779. THOMAS PRYSE, of Cardigan, **Esq.**

1780. HENRY JONES, of Tyglyn, Esq., son of H.S. **for 1734.** He had **one** daughter, who became the second **wife of**

Alban Thomas, Esq., M.D., who practised physic in London, under the auspices of the famous Sir Hans Sloane. Dr. Thomas, on his marriage, assumed the name of Jones; and his son, on the devise to him of the Mynachty estates, adopted that of Gwynne in addition.

1781. DAVID LLOYD, of Allt-yr-odyn, Esq., son of H.S. for 1783.

1782. HERBERT EVANS, of High Mead, Esq.; a member of the family of Glantowy, co. Caermarthen.

1783. JOHN BEYNON, of Trewern, co. Caermarthen, Esq.

1784. WILLIAM WILLIAMS, of Drefach, Esq.

1785. THOMAS POWELL, of Nant-Eos, Esq., only son of the Rev. William Powell, LL.D., of Nant-Eos, by Elizabeth, d. and co-h. of Athelstan Owen, of Rhiwsaeson, co. of Montgomery. He married Elinor, eldest d. of Edward Maurice Corbet, of Ynys-y-maengwyn, co. Merionedd, by whom he had issue two sons and two daughters. This family traces its descent from Howel ab Ieuan, the ninth in descent from Edwin ab Grono, lord of Tegaingl, and founder of the 13th Noble Tribe of North Wales. This Thomas Powell was the eighth in descent from the aforesaid Howel.

1786. EDWARD PRYSE LLOYD, of Glansevin, Esq., son of Morgan Lloyd, Sheriff for Caermarthenshire about 1732. The Lloyds of Glansevin are derived from Idis Wyllt, son of Guthrie, Lord of Desmond, in Ireland, by Nest, his wife, d. of Tydyr Mawr, King of South Wales—Idis, it is said, having come to Wales to assist his uncle, Rhys ab Tydyr, against Bernard Newmarch, in the 11th century, and received the lordship of Llywel, in co. Brecon.

1787. JOHN MARTIN, of Alltgoch, Esq.

1788. JOHN VAUGHAN, of Trewinsor, Esq.

1789. JOHN JONES, of Deri-Ormond, Esq. 2nd time. See 1773.

1790. MATHEW DAVIES, Ynys-hir, Esq. He purchased the estate of Ynys-hir of Mr. Hughes about the year 1780.

He married Jane, d. of H.S. for 1770, and by her had two daughters, who married General Lewes Davies, of Tanybwlch, and Isaac Lloyd Williams, of Lincoln's-Inn, Esq., respectively, and whose grandsons respectively are Mathew L. V. Davies, Esq., of Tanybwlch, and George Griffiths Williams, Esq., of Rhoscellanfawr.

1791. DAVID HUGHES, of Vaenor, Esq.

1792. WILLIAM LEWES, of Llanerchaeron, Esq., eldest son of John Lewes, Esq., by a d. of Thomas Johnes, of Dolau-Cothi. He married Williama, only d. of the Rev. W. Powell, LL.D., of Nant-Eos, by whom he had issue one son and one daughter. He was a descendant of Cadwgan Gràch, lord of Carog, whose Arms were sa. a spear's head, imbrued, between 3 scaling ladders arg., on a chief gu. a tower triple-towered of the second.

1793. THOMAS LLOYD, of Bronwydd, Esq. He was a Captain in the 10th Foot, and subsequently Colonel commanding the Fishguard and Newport Regiment. He married Mary, d. and heiress of John Jones, Esq., M.D., of Haverfordwest, and by her had issue two sons and one daughter.

1794. WILLIAM OWEN BRIGSTOCKE, of Blaenpant, Esq. This family came into Wales from Surrey, and settled first at Llechdwny, in the co. of Caermarthen. On the marriage of William Brigstocke, the H.S. for 1735, with the heiress of — Jenkins, of Blaenpant, the said W. Brigstocke settled at Blaenpant, and the widow of one of his descendants now continues to enjoy the property.

1795. SIR THOMAS BONSALL, of Vronvraith, Knight. He became connected with this county through the lead mines which he so successfully managed for a great number of years. About the year 1784 he purchased the Vronvraith estate of Thomas Morgan, whose father had originally bought it of Mr. Lloyd, of Dan-y-castell.

1796. EDWARD WARREN JONES, of Llanina, Esq., the grandson of H.S. for 1729.

1797. JAMES NATHAN TAYLOR, of Stradmore, Esq.

1798. THOMAS LLOYD, of Coedmawr, Esq., eldest son of H.S. for 1761. He married Elizabeth, fourth d. of Edmund Probyn, Esq., of Newland, by whom he had issue two sons, viz., Thomas (of whom again), and Oliver, who married Anna Maria, only child of Capt. James R. Lewes Lloyd, of Dolhaidd, co. Caermarthen, who had issue two daughters, afterwards married to Captain Thomas Elliott, of Dolhaidd, and W. O. Brigstocke, Esq., of Gellydywyll, respectively. The said Thomas Lloyd had issue also two daughters.

1799. PRYSE LOVEDEN PRYSE, of Gogerddan, Esq. He was the son of Edward Loveden Loveden, of Buscot, co. Berks, by Margaret, d. of Lewis Pryse, of Gogerddan. Mr. Pryse Pryse succeeded to the Buscot property on the death of his father in 1784, and to the estates in Wales on the demise of his mother in 1798, when he also assumed the surname and *arms* of Pryse. He represented the Boroughs of Cardigan in several Parliaments, and married, 1st, in 1798, Harriet, d. of William, second Lord Ashbrook, which lady died *s. p.* in 1813; and 2ndly, Jane, d. of Peter Cavallier, of Gisborough, in Cleveland, by whom he had issue—

1. Pryse Pryse, who afterwards succeeded him to the estates, and was the father of the present Sir Pryse Pryse, Bart. (of whom see 1861).

2. Edward Lewis Pryse, Col. of the Cardiganshire Militia and the present representative of the Cardigan boroughs, and

3. John Pugh Vaughan Pryse, of Bwlchbychan.

1800. THOMAS LLOYD, of Cilgwyn, Esq.

1801. JOHN WILLIAMS, of Castle Hill, Esq., son of H.S. for 1776. He married Mary, the d. of Bowen Jones, of Trewythen, co. Montgomery, and died on the 3rd of May, 1806, leaving his widow, who also died on the 16th

of July, 1825, and an only son (see 1815) him surviving.

1802. DAVID DAVIES, of Glanroca, Esq., derived from Cadivor
ab Dinawal, lord of Castell Hywel. The Glanroca
estate has descended from father to son—the name
being constantly either Jenkin or David—for upwards
of 300 years. The principal seat of this family is at
Maes-y-crugiau, co. Caermarthen.

1803. JOHN LLOYD, of Mabws, Esq.; son of James Lloyd,
of Ffoes-y-bleiddiaid, by Anna Maria, only d. and h.
of Richard Lloyd, of Mabws. John Lloyd was born
in 1753, and married Elinor, the d. and h. of John
Allen, of Dale Castle, co. Pem., by whom he had
issue two sons. The Lloyd family of Ffoes-y-bleiddiaid
is directly descended from Tudwal Gloff, fourth son
of Rhodri Mawr, king of Wales.

1804. JOHN BOND, of Cefn-y-coed, Esq.

1805. JOHN LLOYD WILLIAMS, of Gwernant, Esq.

1806. JOHN BAILY WALLIS, of Peterwell, Esq.; son of Albany
Wallis, who purchased the estate, together with con-
siderable other property in the county, of John Adams,
of Whitland, co. Caermarthen.

1807. THOMAS SMITH, of Norallt, Esq.

1808. MORGAN JONES, of Cilwendeg, Esq. For the pedigree
of this gentleman see under the year 1854.

1809. WILLIAM SKYRME, of Alltgoch, Esq.

1810. WILLIAM EDWARD POWELL, of Nant-Eos, Esq., eldest
son of H.S. for 1785. He was a Col. in the Cardiganshire Militia, and married, 1st., in 1810, Laura
Edwyna, eldest d. of James Sackville-Tufton Phelp,
of Custon House, co. Leicester, by whom he had
two sons, the eldest being the present Col. W. T. R.
Powell, of Nant-Eos; and 2ndly, Harriet Dell, widow
of George Ackers, of Moreton Hall, co. Chester, and
d. of Henry Hoghton, of Cherry Willingham, co.
Lincoln. The *Arms* of the Powells are, Arg. a cross
flory, engr. sa. between 4 Cornish choughs ppr. on a

canton of the 2nd a chev. between three spears'
heads arg. *Crest*, A Talbot's head ppr. collared.
Motto, Inter hastas et hostes.

1811. JOHN BROOKS, of Neuadd-Llanarth, Esq., son of the
Rev. — Brooks, vicar of Llanarth and chaplain to
Dr. Smallwell, Bishop of St. David's. The Rev. Mr.
Brooks married the only daughter of James Griffiths,
of Neuadd-Llanarth, and so became possessed of the
estate.

1812. GRIFFITH JONES, of Cardigan, Esq.

1813. RODERICK EARDLEY RICHARDES, of Pen-y-glais, Esq.,
son of H.S. for 1770. He married Anne Corbetta,
d. of H.S. for 1785.

1814. THOMAS LLOYD, of Bronwydd, Esq., son of H.S. for
1793. He married on the 23rd of July, 1819, Anne
Davies, d. of John Thomas, Esq., of Llwydcoed and
Llettymawr, co. Caermarthen, and died in 1845, leaving issue—

  1. Sir Thomas Davies Lloyd, Bart. : of whom again.
  2. James John Lloyd, m. a d. of late David Arthur Saunders
  Davies, of Pentre, co. Pem., M.P. for co. Cardigan, and has issue.
  3. Rhys Jones Lloyd, in holy orders, m. Anna, d. of T. Lewis
  Lloyd, of Nantgwyllt, co. Radnor, and has issue.
  4. Owen William Lloyd, barrister-at-law, m.
  5. George Martin, *o.s.p.*

1815. JOHN NATHANIEL WILLIAMS, of Castle Hill, Esq., only
son of H.S. for 1801. He was born in 1793, and
married Sarah Elizabeth, second d. of Joseph Loxdale, of Shrewsbury, whom he pre-deceased in 1832.
On the death of Mrs. Williams, in October, 1862, her
brother, James Loxdale, H.S. for 1867, succeeded to
the estate, under her will. The *Arms* of the Wil-
liamses, of Castle Hill, were, Az. a chev. or, between
3 stags' heads, couped. *Crest*, An eagle, ppr. *Motto*,
Pro patria pugna.

1816. THOMAS LLOYD, of Coedmawr, Esq., eldest son of
H.S. for 1798. He married, in 1819, Charlotte,
second d. of the late Capt. Edward Longcroft, R.N.,

of Havant, co. Hants. He was appointed lord-lieutenant and custos rotulorum for the county, and died in 1859, leaving issue—

1. Thomas Edward Lloyd, of Coedmawr, and of the Middle Temple, barrister-at-law, b. April 12, 1820, m., in 1850, Clemena Frances, 2nd d. of the late Rev. David Daniel, and has issue one daughter.

1304190

2. Edmund, b. January 29, 1822, m. and has issue.
3. Walter, b. 7 Dec., 1823.
4. Charles Oliver, b. 9 June, 1825, *o.s.p.*

Arms, Quarterly 1st and 4th sa. a spearhead arg. erect, embrued ppr. between three scaling ladders in bend of the second; 2nd and 3rd, quarterly 1st and 4th ar. a lion ramp. gu. 2nd and 3rd az. a lion ramp. within an orle of quatrefoils. *Crest*, A lion ramp. argent.

1817. JENKIN DAVIES, of Glanrocca, Esq., son of H.S. for 1802.

1818. JOHN JONES, of Deri Ormond, Esq., son of H.S. for 1789. He married Charlotte Elizabeth Jesson, second d. of Thomas Jesson, of Hill Park, co. Kent. An ancestor of Mr. Jesson was knighted on the field of Bosworth for his valour, and the *Crest* which the family now bear, viz., An armed arm, embowed, ppr. holding a rose arg., was conferred upon him on the occasion.

1819. GEORGE JEFFREYS, of Llandovery, Esq.

GEORGE IV.

1820. HENRY ROGERS, of Gelly, Esq.

1821. JOHN VAUGHAN LLOYD, of Tyllwyd, Esq., of the family of Vaughan, of Green-grove, in the vale of Aeron.

1822. THOMAS LEWIS LLOYD, of Nantgwyllt, Esq., eldest son of John Lewis of Gwyndauddwr, by Elizabeth, d. of Thomas Lewis Lloyd, of Nantgwyllt. Mr Lloyd, in the year 1824, assumed by royal licence the surname of Lloyd in addition to that of Lewis; and in 1825 married Elizabeth, d. of Evan Davies, of Trevorgan, Cardigan, Esq., by whom he has issue.

1823. GEORGE WILLIAMS PARRY, of Llidiardau, Esq

1824. JOHN SCANDRETT HARFORD, of Peter's Well, and of
Blaise Castle, co. Gloucester, Esq. He married, in
1812, Louisa, eldest d. of Richard Hart Davies, for
many years M.P. for Bristol ; and was D.C.L. of Ox-
ford, and F.R.S. of London. He contested unsuc-
cessfully the Cardigan Boroughs against Pryse Pryse,
of Gogerddan. *Arms*, Sa. two bends arg. on a
canton az. a bend, or. *Crest*, Out of a coronet
issuing from flames ppr. a griffin's head, or, between
2 wings az. fire issuing from the mouth.

1825. EDWARD PRYSE LLOYD, of Wern-newydd, Esq.

1826. THOMAS DAVIES, The Bridge, Cardigan, Esq. He
married, and had issue two sons, viz., David (of
whom see 1841) and John, who married Letitia, d.
of R. Jones, Esq., of Pantirion, co. Pem., by whom
he had issue Thomas, now of Bank House, Cardigan, J.P., and John (who died in 1866), M.A. of
Jesus Coll., Oxon.

1827. ARTHUR JONES, of Cardigan, Esq.

1828. JOHN GRIFFITH, of Llwyndurus, Esq.

1829. MORRIS DAVIES, of Aberystwith, Esq., a member of
an ancient Merionethshire family, and the first who
established a Bank at Aberystwith.

1830. BENJAMIN HALL, of Cilgwyn, Esq.

WILLIAM IV.

1831. COL. CHICHESTER, of Llanbadarn, great-grandson of
Giles Chichester, of Arlington, co. Devon, whose
widow, Catherine, was interred in the church of
Llanbadarn. See *Meyrick's Cardiganshire.*

1832. EDWARD GWYNNE, of Rhydygors, Esq.

1833. WILLIAM OWEN BRIGSTOCKE, of Blaenpant, Esq. He
married Maria, second d. of the late Admiral William
Henry Webley Parry, of Noyadd-trefawr, a distin-
guished naval officer, and a Knight of the Royal
Swedish Military Order of the Sword. Mr. Brig-

stocke died some years ago, but his widow still lives at Blaenpant.

1834. CHARLES RICHARD LONGCROFT, of Llanina, Esq., son of the late Captain Edward Longcroft, R.N., of Havant, co. Hants. He married, and has issue one son, Charles; and one daughter, Ellen, now married.

1835. THOMAS DAVIES, of Nantywilan, Esq. He married Elizabeth, only d. of Col. Owen Lloyd, of Bronwydd.

1836. GEORGE BOWEN JORDAN JORDAN, of Pigeonsford, Esq., only son of George Price, of Pigeonsford, by Elizabeth, the eldest d. and co-h. of Barret Bowen Jordan, of Neeston, co. Pem. He married, 1st., in July, 1831, Ellen, third d. of Sir John Owen, Bart., of Orielton, co. Pem., and by her had issue two sons, viz., George Price, *o.s.p.*, and Barret Price, and three daughters, viz., Evelyn, Elizabeth Maria, and Angelina; and 2ndly, in 1868, Miss Hall.

Mr. Jordan, whose patronymic was Price, took the name of Jordan under the will of the Rev. John Jordan, of Dumple Dale, co. Pem. *Arms*, Gu. a lion ramp. between eight cross crosslets fitché, or, a chief of the second.

1837. JOHN HUGHES, of Alltlwyd, Esq., son of John Hughes, of Glan'ravon, by Jane Edwards, relict of Thomas Evans, of Llanilar. He m., 1st., in 1833, Mary Anne, eldest d. of Alban T. J. Gwynne, of Mynachty, and by her had an only d., who died an infant; and 2ndly, in 1836, Elizabeth, second d. of G. W. Parry, of Llidiardau, by whom he had issue two sons, John George Parry (of whom see 1864) and William Thomas.

VICTORIA.

1838. WILLIAM TILSLEY JONES, of Gwynvryn, Esq., eldest son of William Jones by Mary, the d. of the Rev. William Tilsley, rector of Penstrowed, and vicar of Llandinam, co. Montgomery; grandson of William

Jones, by his first wife, Jane, the second d. and co-h. of Evan Watkin, of Cynullmawr, and great-grandson of William Jones (son and heir of William John, of Llanbadarn-vawr, who married, in 1690, Jane, second d. of James Jenkins, of the same parish) by a daughter of Thomas Griffiths, of Penbontbren, co. Cardigan. Mr. William Tilsley Jones was born in July, 1782, succeeded his father in 1793, entered the Cardiganshire Militia (of which he became captain and adjutant) in 1803. He married, 1st, in 1821, Jane, d. of Henry Tickell, of Leytonstone, co. Essex; and 2ndly, in 1826, Christiana, sister of his deceased wife. By his first wife he had one son, viz., the Venerable William Basil Jones, M.A., archdeacon of York, and vicar of Bishopsthorpe, co. York—joint author with E. A. Freeman, Esq., of the *History of Saint David's Cathedral*—b. January 2, 1822; m. Sept. 10, 1856, Frances Charlotte, second d. of the late Rev. Samuel Holworthy, M.A., rector of Croxall, co. Derby. Of the second marriage there was issue three daughters, viz., Everard Whiting, Dorothea, and Catherine Emily.

The *Arms* of this family, which are not correctly given in Burke's *Landed Gentry*, are, Arg. a cross flory, between 4 Cornish choughs, sa., armed gu. *Crest*, A demi lion ramp. *Motto*, Mors mihi lucrum.

1839. THE HONORABLE GEORGE VAUGHAN, of Cwmydion.

1840. JOHN LEWES, of Llanaeron, Esq.

1841. DAVID DAVIES, of Castle Green, Esq., eldest son of H.S. for 1726. He married, 1st., Anne Letitia, d. of the Rev. David Griffith, vicar of Nevern, co. Pem., and by her (who died in 1851) had issue two sons, viz., David Griffith, b. in 1835, and Thomas, b. in 1837, *o.s.p.*; and 2ndly, Elizabeth, d. of the Rev. John Holcombe, rector of Cosheton and Rhôscrowther, co. Pem., and prebendary of Brecon.

1842. FRANCIS DAVID SAUNDERS, of Tymawr, Esq., second son of Glanrhydw, co. Caermarthen. He married Mary

Anne, daughter of Rev. George Wade Green, of Court Henry, co. Caermarthen, by whom he had issue two sons and four daughters. He died in the year 1867, leaving his wife and children surviving.

1843. GIBB, of Hendre Velen, or Velin, Esq.

1844. JOHN PHILIPPS ALLEN LLOYD PHILIPPS, of Mabws, Esq., grandson of the H.S. for 1803. He m., in 1823, Charlotte Caroline, youngest d. of the late Capt. William Bartlett, Royal Engineers, and has surviving issue his eldest son, being the present John Allen Lloyd Philipps, of Dale Castle, co. Pem., and Mabws. This gentleman, whose family name originally was Lloyd, assumed the name of Philipps upon the death of Lord Milford, under the will of James Philipps, of Pentypark, Esq., the brother of Mary Lloyd, his great-grandmother. The *Arms* are the same as those of Picton Castle, given in page 3, under the year 1546.

1845. JOHN LLOYD DAVIES, of Blaendyffryn, Esq. He was born in 1801; m., 30 June, 1825, Anne, only surviving child of John Lloyd, Esq. (second son of David Lloyd, of Alltyrodyn), and Elizabeth Lloyd (only child of Philip Lloyd, of Heal-ddu, co. Caermarthen, and had an only child, Arthur Lloyd Davies, b. 1827, who, on attaining his majority took the surname of Lloyd in compliance with his maternal uncle's will. He m. in Dec., 1847, and d. in 1852, leaving a son, John Davies Lloyd, and a daughter, Anne Justina. Mr. John Lloyd Davies served as Member for the co. of Cardigan from A.D. 1855 to 1857, and died in 1860.

1846. JAMES DAVIES, of Ffosrhydgaled, Esq., the nephew and heir of the H.S. for 1829. He married Elizabeth, third daughter of Edward Evans, Esq., and grand-daughter of Pierce Evans, of Upton Castle, co. Pem., Esq., by whom he had issue 5 daughters and one son, Morris Davies, b. 2 March, 1843, educated at Rugby, and called to the Bar, at the Inner Temple, in July, 1867. *Motto*, Y cyfiawn a flodeua (The righteous shall flourish).

1847. MATHEW DAVIES, of Tan-y-bwlch, Esq. The following is the pedigree of this family :—

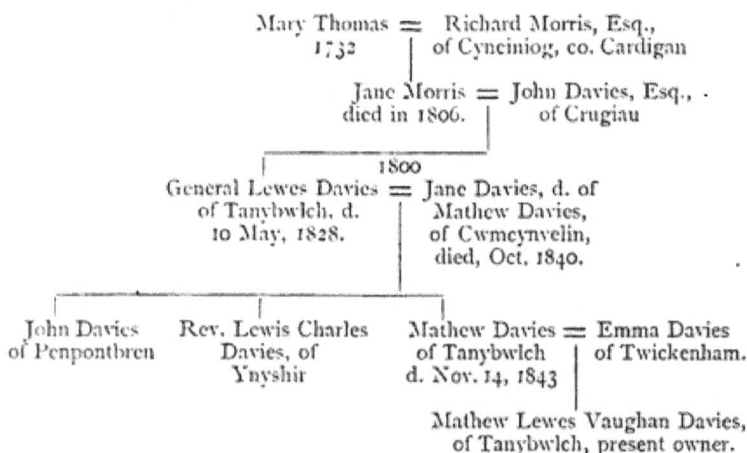

```
            Mary Thomas  ═  Richard Morris, Esq.,
               1732      │    of Cyneiniog, co. Cardigan

                  Jane Morris  ═  John Davies, Esq., ·
                  died in 1806. │     of Crugiau

        ┌─────────────────1800──────────────┐
   General Lewes Davies  ═  Jane Davies, d. of
     of Tanybwlch, d.     │  Mathew Davies,
     10 May, 1828.        │  of Cwmcynvelin,
                          │  died, Oct. 1840.

  ┌──────────┬────────────────┬────────────────┐
John Davies   Rev. Lewis Charles   Mathew Davies  ═  Emma Davies
of Penpontbren   Davies, of        of Tanybwlch   │  of Twickenham.
                 Ynyshir          d. Nov. 14, 1843 │

                              Mathew Lewes Vaughan Davies,
                              of Tanybwlch, present owner.
```

1848. JAMES BOWEN, of Troed-yr-Aur, Esq. *Arms*, Gu. a lion ramp. reguard. or. *Crest*, A nag's head bridled.

1849. HENRY HOUGHTON, of Havod, Esq.

1850. ERNEST AUGUSTUS VAUGHAN, Earl of Lisburne, of Crosswood, eldest son of John, 3rd Earl, by the Hon. Lucy, 5th d. of William, 2nd Viscount Courtenay, m., 1st., in 1835, Mary, d. of the late Sir Laurence Palk, Bart.; 2ndly, in 1853, Harriet Elizabeth, d. of the late Col. Henry Hugh Mitchell. His heir apparent is Ernest Augustus Mallet, Viscount Vaughan, of Birch Grove, co. Cardigan, m., in 1858, Gertrude, 3rd d. of Edwin Burnaby, Esq., of Baggrave Hall, co. Leicester, by whom he has issue.

1851. THOMAS DAVIES LLOYD, of Bronwydd, Esq., created a Baronet in 1863. The eldest son of H.S. for 1814, b. in 1820, m. Henrietta Mary, fourth d. of George Reid, Esq., of Bunker's Hill and Friendship Estates, Jamaica, by Louisa, d. of Sir Charles Oakeley, Bart., by whom he has issue one son, viz., Marteine Owen Mowbray, b. 8 Feb., 1851. Sir Thomas is the 23rd

Lord of the Barony of Kemes in hereditary descent from Martin de Tours, one of the companions in arms of William the Conqueror. The Barony of Kemes is the only "Lordship Marcher" now in existence in the kingdom, and the lords thereof still exercise a portion of their rights and annually appoint under their seal the mayor of Newport, Pem. The Barons of Kemes were formerly summoned by writ to Parliament, and there is evidence that the first seven Barons sat there by virtue of their barony and writ. For a full pedigree of this family, prepared by Sir Thomas Phillipps, Bart., I would refer the reader to the *Archæologia Cambrensis. Arms*, Az. a wolf salient arg. *Crest*, A boar chained to a holly bush ppr. *Motto*, I Ddaw bo'r diolch.

1852. LEWIS PUGH, of Abermaed, Esq. He died a short time ago. *Crest*, A lion ramp. holding in his forepaw a spear's head.

1853. JOHN INGLIS JONES, of Deri-Ormond, Esq., son of H.S. for 1818. He m. in August, 1860, the Lady Elizabeth Malet Vaughan, eldest d. of the Earl of Lisburne, and has three children living, viz., Mary Gwendolen Inglis, Herbert Inglis, and Wilmot Inglis. Mr. Jones bears for *Arms* those of Ednowain Bendew, founder of one of the fifteen Noble Tribes of North Wales, from whom he traces his descent, viz., Arg. a chev. between three boars' heads couped sa. Having been elected Sheriff against his remonstrances, and being at the time an officer on full pay in the Royal Horse Guards, he only served the office at one Assizes, and having resigned—

ALBAN LEWES THOMAS JONES GWYNNE, of Mynachty, Esq., was appointed as a substitute. Mr. Gwynne (since dead) was a Captain in the 62nd Regiment. He m., in 1847, Jane Crawshay, d. of Crawshay Bailey, Esq., M.P., of Nantyglo, co. Monmouth, and had issue two sons, viz., 1. Alban; 2. Arthur, d. Feb.,

1860; and three daughters, viz., 1. Gertrude Jane;
2. Agnes: and 3. Edith. (See *Burke's Landed Gentry.)*
1854. MORGAN JONES, of Pen-y-lan, Esq., nephew of H.S. for
1808. The following is the pedigree of this family:—

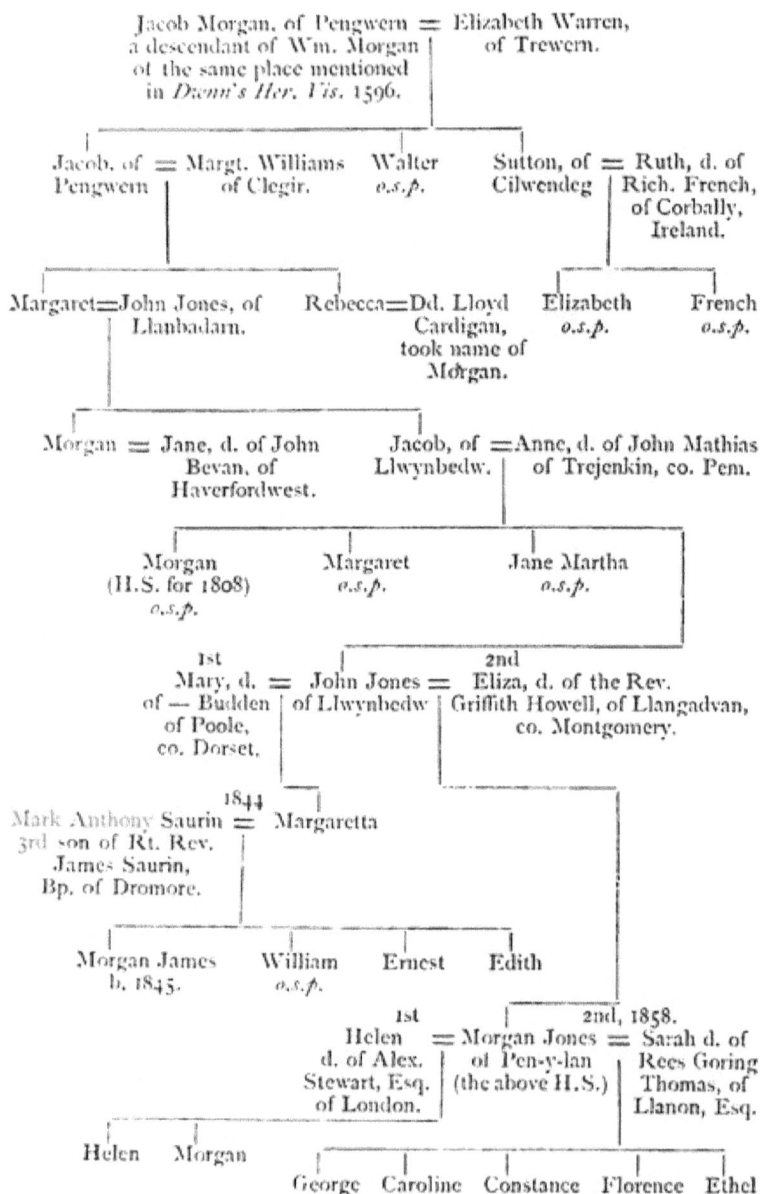

Jacob Morgan, of Pengwern, = Elizabeth Warren,
a descendant of Wm. Morgan | of Trewern.
of the same place mentioned
in *Dwnn's Her. Vis.* 1596.

Jacob, of = Margt. Williams   Walter   Sutton, of = Ruth, d. of
Pengwern | of Clegir.   *o.s.p.*   Cilwendeg | Rich. French,
                                              of Corbally,
                                              Ireland.

Margaret=John Jones, of   Rebecca=Dd. Lloyd   Elizabeth   French
       | Llanbadarn.   Cardigan,   *o.s.p.*   *o.s.p.*
                             took name of
                             Morgan.

Morgan = Jane, d. of John   Jacob, of =Anne, d. of John Mathias
       Bevan, of   Llwynbedw. | of Trejenkin, co. Pem.
       Haverfordwest.

      Morgan   Margaret   Jane Martha
   (H.S. for 1808)   *o.s.p.*   *o.s.p.*
      o.s.p.

      1st   2nd
  Mary, d. = John Jones = Eliza, d. of the Rev.
of — Budden | of Llwynbedw | Griffith Howell, of Llangadvan,
  of Poole,   co. Montgomery.
  co. Dorset.

           1844
Mark Anthony Saurin = Margaretta
3rd son of Rt. Rev. |
  James Saurin,
  Bp. of Dromore.

Morgan James   William   Ernest   Edith
  b. 1845.   *o.s.p.*

           1st   2nd, 1858.
       Helen = Morgan Jones = Sarah d. of
    d. of Alex. | of Pen-y-lan | Rees Goring
   Stewart, Esq. | (the above H.S.) | Thomas, of
   of London.   Llanon, Esq.

Helen   Morgan   George   Caroline   Constance   Florence   Ethel

1855. JOHN BATTERSBY HARFORD, of Falcondale, Esq., eldest son of the late Abraham Gray Harford (who assumed the name of Battersby by Royal licence) by Elizabeth, d. of Major-General and Lady Eleanor Dundas, of Carron Hall, co. Stirling; m., in 1850, Mary Charlotte Elizabeth, d. of the late Baron de Bunsen.

1856.   WINWOOD, of Tyglyn, Esq.

1857. JOHN PROPERT, of Blaenpistyll, Esq., the only son of Thomas Propert, Esq., of Blaenpistyll, co, Cardigan. He was born on the 19th July, 1793, and having chosen physics as his profession, he became a perpetual pupil of the celebrated Abernethy in Oct., 1811. In 1814 he gained his diploma, and having selected London as the scene of his labours, he started on a prosperous career, and established an excellent practice. His name has for many years been associated with several benevolent undertakings, the most important of which was his promoting the foundation of the Royal Medical Benevolent College and Asylum at Epsom, which was first projected by him in 1851, and opened in 1855. This institution serves as an asylum for such medical men as have from ill health or other adverse influences sunk into poverty, and for the widows of medical men in reduced circumstances. In connection with it also is a school for the gratuitous education of the orphans of medical men. Mr. Propert married, in Sept., 1824, Julia Anne, only daughter of Robert Ross, of Cork, solicitor, and died in Sept. 1867, leaving issue three sons and four daughters, viz. :—

     1. John Lumsden, of Gloucester Place, Portman Square, surgeon, m. in April, 1864, Jesica Mary, eldest d. of W. S. P. Hughes, of Powick, co. Worcester, solicitor.

     2. William Henry, in the Bombay Civil Service.

     3. Frederick Norman Griffith.

     1. Sophia Jane, m. in April, 1852, E. Norton Clifton, of Harley Street, Cavendish Square, architect.

2. Juliana ; 3. Harriett ; and 4. Mary Gordon, m. July, 1864, Wharton P. Hood, of Upper Berkeley Street, Portman Square, Esq., M.D.

1858. THOMAS HUGHES, of Noyadd-vawr, Esq.

1859. WILLIAM LEWES, of Llysnewydd, Esq., eldest son of the late William Lewes, of Llysnewydd, by Williama Anne, d. of William Lewis, Esq., of Llanayron, m., in 1837, Anna, d. of James Beatty, Esq., M.D., of Enniskillen, Fermanagh, and has issue.

1860. WILLIAM JONES, of Glandenis, and also of Llwyndu, co. Caermarthen, Esq., the second son of John Jones, Blaen-nos, grandson of David Jones, of Pantglas, Esq., and grand-nephew of Col. Williams of Henllys, co. Caermarthen. The estates now possessed by Mr. Jones have been in the possession of the family for over three centuries. *Arms*, Gu. 3 stags' heads, erased, arg. between a chevron arg., thereon a falcon, ppr. *Crest*, A bull's head ppr. bezantee.

1861. PRYSE LOVEDEN, of Gogerddan, Esq. (now Sir Pryse Pryse, Bart.), eldest son of the late Pryse Loveden, Esq., of Buscot Park, Berks, and of Gogerddan (who was M.P. for the Cardigan Boroughs, 1847—1855). He married, in 1859, Louisa Jane, youngest d. of Captain Lewes, of Llanllyr, by whom he has issue. He resumed the family name of Pryse by Royal licence in 1863, and was created a Baronet in 1866.

1862. HERBERT VAUGHAN, of Brynog, Esq., eldest son of the late Col. Herbert Vaughan, of Llangoedmore ; m., in 1862, Julia, only child of the Rev. Lewis Davies, of Ynyshir, co. Cardigan. This family is a younger branch of that of the Earl of Lisburne.

1863. PRICE LEWIS, of Gwastod, Esq.

1864. JOHN GEORGE PARRY HUGHES, of Alltlwyd, Esq., eldest son of H.S. for 1837, by Elizabeth, d. of George William Parry, of Llidiardau.

1865. JOHN LEWES, of Llanllyr, Lieut.-Col., m. a daughter of the Rev. Charles Griffith, brother to John Griffith, Esq., of Llwyndurus.

1866. JOHN GEORGE WILLIAM BONSALL, of Fronfraith, Esq., second son of the Rev. Isaac Bonsall, M.A., Rector of Llanwnin, co. Montgomery, by Catherine, d. of the late Rev. John Davies, Rector of Cemmaes, same county, and grandson of the late Sir Thomas Bonsall, H.S. for 1795, by Winifred Williams, d. of Isaac Williams, Esq., of Fronfraith. Mr. Bonsall m., in 1853, Frances, d. of the late Joseph Davies, Esq., of Gallt-y-llan, co. Montgomery, and has issue.

1867. JAMES LOXDALE, of Castle Hill, Esq., third son of Joseph Loxdale, who for upwards of half a century was High Steward and Deputy Recorder of the borough of Shrewsbury, by Anna Maria, d. of William Wood of Bayston, co. Salop. Mr. Loxdale was born on the 7th Oct. 1747, and is an M.A. of St. John's Coll., Cantab. He is slso a Magistrate and Deputy-Lieutenant for the counties of Stafford, Salop, and Cardigan. Succeeded to the Castle Hill estate by devise under the will of his sister, Sarah Elizabeth Williams, the widow of the H.S. for 1815, on her decease on the 14th Oct., 1862.

This family traces its descent from ROBERT LOXDALE, who lived at Mere Town, parish of Ferton, co. of Stafford, his own estate by inheritance, in the time of Henry VIII. He married Joan Undyrwood, by whom he had one son.

MICHAEL, of Mere Town, who married in 1559 Alice Gretbacke, and died in April, 1594, leaving 2 sons and 3 daughters. His eldest son,

ROBERT, of Mere Town (baptized on the 27th Dec., 1564), married Winifred ———, by whom he had issue three daughters and one son, named

THOMAS, of Mere Town (bap. 19 Sept., 1599) who married Sarah Worthington (buried 22 July, 1655). The issue of this marriage consisted of 3 sons and 7 daughters. The eldest son,

JOHN, also of Mere Town, born in 1643, married, and had issue,

1. Thomas, of Trin. Coll., Cantab., M.A., born Dec. 3, 1675, vicar of Seighford and rector of Ferton, co. Stafford, which he

resigned in 1721, and became vicar of Leek, which he also resigned in 1735 and became rector of Tixal—"a man of learning and fond of antiquarian researches." He was the author of *Parochial Anti-quities of Staffordshire* and other local histories in MSS. cited in *Shaw's Staffordshire*, &c. He married Elizabeth, d. of Francis Eld, of Seighford, Esq., but had no issue.

2. Richard, born Oct., 1680, *o.s.p.* January 7, 1732. He was the first of the family who settled at Shrewsbury, where he practised as a solicitor. He was an ensign in the "Artilary Regiment raised voluntarily by the inhabitants in the year 1715 in opposition to the rebels," under Lord Viscount Newport.

3. Joseph, of whom again, and
Two other sons and two daughters.

JOSEPH, the above named, born on the 8th January, 1682, settled at Stafford, of which place he was Mayor in 1745, and married Mary Thorley, a relation to William, of Wykeham, the founder of Winchester and New Coll., by whom he had issue

1. Thomas, of whom again.

2. Joseph, *o.s.p.*

3. Anne, who died in Oct., 1791, having married Richard Warren, of Stafford, leaving issue three sons and one daughter.

THOMAS, the eldest son of Joseph, born 29 July, 1720, was Mayor of Shrewsbury for 1774, and died April 20, 1793, having married Hannah Skite, by whom he had issue,

1. Mary, b. 1754, who married the Rev. Thomas Eden, M.A., rector of Alvercott, Oxon, and Illmington, co. Warwick, and had issue William Henry Loxdale, born August 10, 1783.

2. Anne, who married the Rev. Thomas Coke, of Jesus Coll., Oxon, D.C.L., author of a Commentary on the Bible, a friend of Wesley and an active member of the Wesleyan Conference.

3. Thomas, born 3 April, 1757, died 25 January, 1842. A magistrate and D.L. for Salop. He married his cousin, Deborah Warren, by whom he had one d., Anne, who also married her cousin, John Loxdale.

4. Joseph, of whom again.

5. Sarah, born Dec. 1762, married the Rev. Thomas Hill, of Alcaston Manor, co. Salop, curate of Crosby, co. Lancaster, and chaplain to Clodius, Lord Bishop of Sodor and Man. She died *s.p.*

6. Richard, born March, 1769, and died April, 1848, having married Jane Jeffrey, sister of the H.S. for 1819, leaving four sons.

JOSEPH, the second son of the above named Thomas, born the 12 August, 1759, married Anna Maria Wood, as aforesaid. He was Mayor of Shrewsbury in 1797, and died the 2nd of April, 1846, having had issue,

1. Thomas Wood, b. 1791; *o.s.p.* 1837.

2. Anna Maria, b. April, 1792; d. June, 1863, having married

the Rev. Frederick Holmes, Professor at Bishop's Coll., Calcutta, by whom she had three sons and one daughter.

3. **Joseph, b.** August, 1793. Mayor of Shrewsbury, 1830, *o.s.p.* March, 1838.

4. Sarah Elizabeth, b. Dec., 1795, m. John Nathaniel Williams, of Castle Hill. H.S. 1815. She died Oct., 14, 1862, having devised her estate at Castle Hill to her brother,

5. JAMES, the H.S. for 1867 as aforesaid.

6. John, b. Aug. 1799, m., 1st, his cousin, **Anne** Loxdale, **who** died without issue, July, 1848; 2ndly, **Anna Shee** Watson, d. **of** the Rev. John Watson, D.D , vicar of **Ringford** cum Deuford and Great Dodington, co. Northampton, by whom he had issue, John **Watson,** Mary Jane, Geoffrey Walter Peele, and Reginald James. She died in January, 1860, and Mr. Loxdale married, 3rdly, Jane Phillips Bradley, widow of — Bradley, **Esq., of** Lombard Street, London.

7. Henrietta Sophia, b. April, 1802, *o.s.p.* 1842.

8. George Henry, b. March, 1804, m. Sarah Bagot, d. of his **Honor George** Bagot, H.S. of British Guiana, by whom he has issue three sons and five daughters.

9. Charlotte Emilia, b. January, 1806, *o.s.p.* 1831.

10. Richard **Skite,** died an infant.

11. Emma Louiza, b. Feb. 1809

12. Laura Matilda, b. April, 1812, *o.s.p.* Oct. 1829.

1868. ALBAN THOMAS DAVIES, of Tyglyn, Esq.

ADDENDA ET CORRIGENDA.

Page 11, 1604. *Descendant*, in the fourth line, should be *ancestor*.

,, ,, 1607. *Ystrad Eflur*, should be *Ystrad Fflur*.

,, 23, 1676. *Since*, should be *afterwards*.

,, 27, 1770. This John Morgan was a descendant of David Morgan, of Plas, Aberporth, and a brother of the Rev. David Morgan, of Cardigan, incumbent of Randleston, Ireland, from whom the present Thomas Morgan, of Cardigan, Esq., is descended.

,, 28, 1770. Roderick Richardes was the grandson of Roderick the son of Richard Rhydderch. The house of Penglais was erected by the H.S. for 1699.

,, 30, 1781. For the year 1783, read 1743.

,, 31, 1792. For *Lewes*, read *Lewis*. Llanerchaeron is now called Llanaeron.

,, 38, 1840. *John Lewes*, should be *John William Lewis*. He was the only son of William Lewis, of Llanaeron, and married in May, 1841, Mary Ashby Mettam, 2nd d. of the Rev. George Mettam, rector of Barwell, co. Leicester. He died *s.p.* the 4th July, 1855.

,, ,, 1841. For 1726, read 1826.

,, 39, 1843. The sheriff's name was Francis.

MORGAN & DAVIES, "WELSHMAN" PRINTING OFFICE, CARMARTHEN.

FURTHER NOTES.

—o—

BLAENPANT AND NOYADD-TREVAWR.

JOHN PARRY, the H.S. for 1620, was the son of the H.S. for 1604, by his wife Maud, d. & h. of Llew. ap David ap Llewelyn of Blaenpant (*L. Dwnn* 1, p 56). He died while in office, and his father completed his term.

DAVID PARRY, H.S. for 1630, was the eldest son of the above John Parry, and succeeded to the estates on the death of his grandfather, the H.S. for 1604.

DAVID PARRY, H.S. for 1685, was the son of David (who married his cousin Elizabeth, d. of Thomas Parry, of St. Dogmaels), and grandson of John Parry, brother to H.S. for 1630. He died *s.p.* in 1711.

STEPHEN PARRY, H.S. for 1720, was the eldest son of John Parry, and grandson of John Parry, the brother of the H.S. for 1630. Stephen married his cousin Ann, d. of David Parry, by Elizabeth, d. of Thomas Parry, of St. Dogmaels, and died in 1724, *s.p.*

DAVID PARRY, H.S. for 1745, was a nephew of H.S. for 1720, being son of William Parry of Nevern, by Susan, the Sister of the said Stephen Parry. David Parry married Frances, d. & h. of Kedgwin Webley of Broadham's Court, co. Gloucester, and had issue Frances (*o.s.p.* 1816), who married Marmaduke Gwyn of Garth, co. Brecon. She devised her estate to her cousin, William Henry Webley, Rear Admiral, C.B., &c., who thereupon assumed the name and arms of Parry. He died at Noyadd in 1837, having married Maria Washington, only daughter of John White of Larne, co. Antrim, by whom he had (among other issue) William Henry Webley, who married Catherine Angharad, d. of David Davies of Pentre, by whom he had (among other issue) David Kedgwin Webley Parry, now living (1868).

BLAENPANT AND LLECHDWNY.

The first member of the Brigstocke family who settled in Wales was John Brigstocke, who m. Mary, d. of David Morris Bowen, of Llechdwny. This John Brigstocke purchased Llechdwny of his father-in-law. He had issue Owen, who married Jane, d. of Sir William Vaughan, of which marriage there was issue one son, William, who married Winifred, d. of Robert Birt, Mayor of Carmarthen in 1698. Owen, the eldest son of

William, dying without issue, William, the second son, succeeded to the property. He was a barrister-at-law, and married Elizabeth d. of William Jenkins, of Carrog and of Blaenpant, by Bridget, d. of James Lewis of Gelly-dywyll. William Jenkins's father was Reginald Jenkins of Carrog, who had obtained Blaenpant through his marriage with Eleanor, d. of David Parry of Noyadd. William, the eldest son of the said William Brigstocke by Elizabeth Jenkins, married Mary, d. of Francis Lloyd of Glyn (or Mumbles—*Golden Grove Book*), by whom he had issue Owen, who married Ann, d. of John Williams of Bwlchgwynt. The issue of this Marriage was William Owen Brigstocke, the H.S. for 1794, who married Anne Probyn, of Newland, by whom he had four sons and four daughters, viz. :

1. William, m. 1st, Harriet, d. of Sir Wiliam Mausel, of Muddlescombe, Bart., and 2ndly, Maria, third d. of Rear Admiral William Henry Webley Parry, of Noyadd-trevawr. He died *s.p.*
2. John.
3. Augustus, m. Jane Anne Bridget, d. of David Davies, of Pentre, by whom he had issue Wm. Owen Brigstocke, of Gellydywyll, now living (1868).
4. Robert.
1. Anne.
2. Sophia, m. ——— Buck, barrister-at-law, whose only son, William Buck, now resides at Stradmore (1868.)
3. Caroline, m. Rev. John Stanley. Their daughter Harriette m. James Bevan Bowen, of Llwyngwair, M.P. for Pembrokeshire.
4. Eliza, m. Major Henry Leach, of Corston.

COEDMAWR.

JAMES LEWIS, of Cileyffeth, the H.S. for 1645, was of Coedmawr. He became possessed of Cileyffeth in right of his wife, the widow of David Lloyd of that place. He was High Sheriff for the co. of Pembroke in 1641.

GOGERDDAN.

SIR RICHARD PRYSE, the H.S. for 1655, was the eldest son and heir of the H S. for 1639. His widow, Elizabeth, d. to Sir Bulstrode Whitlock, m. 2ndly John Herbert, a younger son of Havod, who on his marriage went to reside at Gogerddan, and was H.S. for this county in 1684. [*Golden Grove Book.*]

www.ingramcontent.com/pod-product-compliance
Lightning Source LLC
Chambersburg PA
CBHW021522090426
42739CB00007B/727